BY WOR

AND DE:

THE DECADE OF EVANGELISM

By Word and Deed

Sharing the Good News through Mission

Edited by Colin Craston

Published for the Anglican Communion
by CHURCH HOUSE PUBLISHING

ISBN 0 7151 4822 2

Published 1992 for the Anglican Communion Office,
Partnership House, 157 Waterloo Road, London SE1 8UT

by Church House Publishing,
Church House, Great Smith Street, London SW1P 3NZ

Typeset by BPCC Techset Ltd, Exeter
Printed in Great Britain by BPCC Wheatons Ltd, Exeter

CONTENTS

SECTION II
MISSION IN CONTEXT: CHURCH AND WORLD

SECTION III
MOVEMENT TO MISSION: A MASSIVE SHIFT

FOREWORD

Robert Renouf

The Lambeth Conference 1988 called on the Member Churches of the Anglican Communion, in co-operation with other Christians, to make the closing years of this millennium a Decade of Evangelism. Recognising evangelism as the primary task given to the Church, the bishops called for a renewal and united emphasis on making Christ known to the people of his world. At their meeting in Cyprus in April of 1989, the Primates of the Communion affirmed this call. A new vision of mission was called for, a holistic mission in which evangelism is a central component. In his essay David Winter writes that 'mission without evangelism is incomplete and evangelism without mission is impoverished.' *By Word and Deed: Sharing the Good News Through Mission* is written with bishops and other evangelism leaders, lay and ordained, in mind. The authors explore the components, contexts and priorities of mission and their relationship to the centrality of evangelism.

There are considerable differences throughout the Church regarding the meaning of mission and also the meaning of evangelism. Most Christians, however, believe that the Church has a God-given task that can be termed mission. An increasing number of Christians also believe that mission takes place most effectively when the Great Commission and the Great Commandment are carried out by the Church engaging in total interface with the world. The dynamic components of mission have been identified as proclamation, nurture, service, transformation, evangelism, and integrity of creation. These complementary components relate to each other, each is indispensable and none is interchangeable. Evangelism, as one of these components, is seen as being central to mission, as mission is central to the ministry of the Church. However, when any component is neglected or missing, mission becomes thwarted, hindered, or in extreme situations, impossible. For mission to be effective all its components must be working together to express the Good News that 'God so loved the world' and that God still loves the world. Jesus was sent by the Father to convert God's vision into today's mission. This book is about evangelism and that mission.

The authors address the six components of mission and their relationships to evangelism, to each other and to the world. They explore mission in cultural, socio-political, and ecumenical contexts and how the mission components are affected by these phenomena. They also examine what is required in terms of viable structures, effective training and strategies for a massive shift from maintenance to mission to take place. The key role of laity is given specific attention. The whole people of God are called, as members of the Church, to become agents of mission in the world during the Decade of Evangelism in the closing years of this millennium. *By Word and Deed: Sharing the Good News Through Mission* is an evangelistic tool to help leaders of the Decade reflect critically upon mission in light of the Gospel.

The book is a concrete expression of mission partnership in action. The Member Churches have every reason to express their deepest appreciation to the writers without whose efforts this book would not be available to help Church leaders carry forth mission during the Decade of Evangelism. We are indebted to each of the authors. There is another group to whom we are also indebted, for without their financial support *By Word and Deed* would not have been published. I refer to Church Missions Publishing Company of the Episcopal Diocese of Connecticut (ECUSA) and its Bishop, the Rt Revd Arthur E. Walmsley, President of the Board of Managers. For over 100 years this small mission society has helped publish materials to aid in the advance of Christian mission and to further the cause of foreign mission in the Anglican Church throughout the world. Funding *By Word and Deed* is part of its missionary outreach of sharing the Word, a goal to which it has remained constant. We offer our deepest thanks to Bishop Walmsley and the Church Missions Publishing Company for being mission partners with the Anglican Consultative Council and the various authors in making possible this project. For more information about the Church Missions Publishing Company, write to the Rt Revd Arthur E. Walmsley, 1335 Asylum Avenue, Hartford, Connecticut 06105, USA.

LIST OF CONTRIBUTORS

The Revd Canon Dr Robert W. Renouf, ACC Adviser, Decade of Evangelism, 1989-91.

The Revd Canon Colin Craston, Chairman of the Anglican Consultative Council.

The Revd David Winter, Bishop's Officer for Evangelism in the Diocese of Oxford, England, and a former Head of Religious Broadcasting at the BBC.

Dr Janet Hodgson, USPG Area Secretary for the Diocese of Oxford, England, and formerly in the Department of Religious Studies in the University of Capetown.

The Rt Revd Dr James H. Ottley, Bishop of Panama.

The Revd Canon Kenyon E. Wright, Director of the Kairos Centre, Glasgow.

The Rt Revd Dr Alexander John Malik, Bishop of Lahore, Church of Pakistan.

The Most Revd French Chang-Him, Archbishop of the Province of the Indian Ocean.

The Revd Dr Jaci Maraschin, Priest of the Igreja Episcopal do Brasil and Professor of Theology in the Post-Graduate Programme on Science of Education in Sao Paolo.

The Very Revd Dr James C. Fenhagen, Dean of the General Theological Seminary, New York.

The Revd Canon Dr Sehon Goodridge, Principal of the Simon of Cyrene Theological Institute, Wandsworth, London.

The Rt Revd Yong Ping Chung, Bishop of Sabah, East Malaysia.

The Rt Revd Roger A. Herft, Bishop of Waikato, New Zealand.

The Rt Revd Gideon I. Oladipo Olajide, Bishop of Ibadan, Nigeria.

AN INTRODUCTION AND A PLEA

Colin Craston

It was a privilege to take over responsibility for editing this series of essays from Robert Renouf when his time as Adviser for the Decade of Evangelism came to an end. On behalf of the Anglican Consultative Council I pay tribute to him for all he did in stimulating response across the Communion and enabling the sharing of resources for the Decade. In his letter of invitation to the prospective authors he saw this book as one of those resources, the need for which had become clear from his contacts and correspondence with member Churches.

I extend my own grateful thanks to the authors for their work and for their kind co-operation. For some English is not their first language, or even their second. In all inter-Anglican communication and consultation greater attention is being paid to provision of multi-language facilities, but as yet English has to be the medium for this kind of book.

Culture and Theology

The essays reveal a wide diversity of culture and of theological and missiological understanding. Rather late in the spread of the Gospel and the Church across the world have we realised the significance of culture. Much damage followed the insensitive displacement of indigenous cultures and the import of Western culture as though of the essence of the Gospel, as Christianity came to new areas. Only gradually is the damage being remedied.

When, however, emphasis is given to God as Creator and Sustainer, as well as Redeemer, culture is seen as part of his manifold provision for human life. The Good News of Jesus Christ affirms what is good in culture, while also judging what is contrary to the Kingdom and redeeming what must be changed. To think otherwise would be to deny the possibility of God's rule now on earth. And so, the presentation, though not the essential content of the Gospel, must differ from culture to culture. A major task in the Decade of Evangelism is to discover ways of presentation relevant to each culture. What questions are being asked? What needs felt? What view of life underlies behaviour? These are the kind of concerns to be faced, always remembering, however, that ultimately the most important question is that put to human beings by God—What will you do about Christ? Culture may determine how the agenda is presented, but it does not determine its contents.

As well as writing from their own culture the authors, the editor included, approach the challenge of the Decade of Evangelism from their own missiological perceptions. These essays reflect the considerable diversity of reaction within the Anglican Communion to the Lambeth Conference call for the Decade. It cannot be otherwise, if evangelism cannot be isolated from all else that is involved in the mission of the Church. Mission can only be compartmentalised in discussion not in practice, even though at any given time and in any situation one aspect occupies attention and energies. The Lambeth Fathers recognised this as they made their call. They were clear that evangelism meant 'proclamation of salvation through faith in Christ with a view to making new Christians' and that the unevangelised were 'not only those who have not been baptised', and, as they also said, the 'lapsed' who have fallen away from commitment to Christ and his Church, 'but also those who have never even been touched by the Gospel'.[1] Yet they went on to say 'We can see few better ways by which the quality and diversity of the ministry of the whole of our Church could be enhanced than by a new determination to evangelise. We believe that upon this foundation, other aspects of mission, as for example in the relief of need, the revision of unjust structures of society, or the transforming of the levels of human existence, must no less painstakingly be built'.[2] Such anxieties about the Decade as spring from missiological convictions relate to the determination and ability of Anglicans, and other fellow Christians, to engage in mission across all its range, as well as giving a new emphasis to evangelism.

To avoid the Lord's judgment on his Church being 'This you should have done, and not left the other undone', it is essential to bear in mind what the Church is in the world for, as she moves through the Decade. Worship, ministry and mission are three words to sum up the Church's calling. They are inextricably linked, but if the first two mainly apply to what happens within the community of faith, the third relates to the world in which the Church is set.

What is the Church For?

Understanding of mission, its meaning and effective prosecution, requires a sound ecclesiology, for the Church is an indispensable part of the Gospel. The Good News of God's love and action in Christ includes his calling into being of the Church, a new race of redeemed men and women, as a sign, instrument and foretaste or earnest of his Kingdom. Since the ultimate purpose of God's Kingdom is the reconciliation of all things in Christ, the Church itself must be seen as a reconciled community. Anything less in any place undermines its credibility in witness to the reconciliation Christ has won and offers. It may, and should, reflect in its life all the diversity of humanity redeemed and reconciled.

Furthermore, since the Kingdom of God brings in a reign of righteousness, justice and peace, the Church must manifest those qualities within its communal life, and work for their promotion in society at large, and thus for its transformation, or again its credibility is undermined. In order to *do* what it is called to do in mission, the Church must *be* what it is called to be.

Mission and Evangelism

Mission has been described within Anglican circles as 'the reconciliation of man (sic) to God, man to man, and man to his environment'. Successive documents produced by Anglican consultative bodies have emphasised what the reconciliation of men and women to God requires from the Church. 'Evangelism is the faithful proclamation of the Gospel, the Church's witness to Jesus Christ in the power of the Holy Spirit by word and deed, which faces humanity with the inescapable choice of making a decision. It is a clear call to repentance, trust in Jesus Christ as Saviour, and commitment to serve him in the fellowship of the Church'.[3] 'The work of the Church in preaching the Gospel, baptising and building up a visible fellowship is integral to the mission of God'.[4] 'Evangelism is the proclamation of the historical, biblical Christ as Saviour and Lord, with a view to persuading people to come to him personally and so be reconciled to God, to one another and to creation'.[5] These are some of the affirmations made over the years.

Much thought then has been given to mission and the place of evangelism in mission, to the concept of reconciliation as the heart of mission and to the Church's calling to be a witness to and example of God's reconciliation, the ultimate goal of which is the unity of all things in Christ. Where there seems to me to be a serious lack of contemporary thought concerns the basis on which all the reconciliation is grounded—the death and resurrection of Jesus Christ. The Cross, standing for Christ crucified and risen, is the very heart of the Good News. How do we understand and present it today—especially in all those cultures where biblical categories and images are indeed a foreign language. There is no reconciliation of men and women to God without the Cross, no hope for the reconciliation of all things except as a result of what was accomplished at the Cross.

A Theology of the Cross

As I have argued elsewhere, the time is ripe to redress an imbalance in Anglican theology.[6] Since the *Lux Mundi* essays incarnational theology has had a dominant influence. Without neglect of the gains that have flowed from that emphasis, a new attention to the meaning of the atonement and its cosmic significance is required. The Decade of Evangelism increases the urgency of the task. The Good News is centred on God's love in Christ and his act of reconciliation through the Cross, but we cannot assume people will understand the necessity for the Cross. They need a credible and convincing presentation.

I will presume to sketch a few outlines of what I believe is required by way of stimulating others more competent in theology. First, we need to explore what it means to speak of God not just as Love, but as Holy Love. He is absolute moral perfection and goodness, a God of justice and righteousness, who must at all costs uphold his moral reign over the universe, or cease to be God. Holiness is not just an attribute, it is his essence, as much as love is. Unless we acknowledge him as absolutely holy there is the risk of our attempts to understand his love degenerating into a sentimentality that is indifferent to the moral gulf that exists between man and God. While we know that all love has its origin in God, we need to avoid talking of his love in purely anthropomorphic terms, for in his holiness he is 'wholly other'.

Listening to Yesterday's Theologians

I will freely admit my debt in understanding to theologians of previous generations in the twentieth century, mostly from non-Anglican traditions, but the longer I go on in pastoral ministry the more I am convinced of the abiding relevance of much of what they say about the Cross. Indeed, the more remote certain biblical images—blood, justification, the Lamb, for instance—seem to modern ears, the more we must concentrate on categories emphasised by the theologians I am referring to. Categories such as perfection, goodness, justice, morality are still valid currency with many, even though they recognise their own falling short.

The Good News of God cannot be truly presented without the element of 'bad news'. There is a moral gulf between all in the human race and a holy God. And it is not explained simply in terms of ignorance, dullness, weakness of a creature in relation to the Creator, but it is, essentially, a state of self-centred independence over against God, resulting in disobedience and a flouting of his moral reign.

Emil Brunner spoke of God creating man out of love and for love. And man can only find his true destiny and freedom when he is in that love. The Benedictus speaks of us becoming 'free to worship him without fear: holy and righteous in his sight all the days of our life'. But because of sin—a state not just an act—man cannot by his own achievement attain a right relationship to a holy God, cannot bridge the gulf. Indeed God's holiness makes a total demand, a total claim which man in his highest moments may recognise but totally fail to meet.

'The truth of Christianity must rest on a view of life which starts from the primacy and finality of the moral, recognises the wreck of the moral, and presents the grand problem as the restitution of the moral'.[7] Thus a great theologian, P. T. Forsyth, described as 'a man before his time', introduces the Gospel agenda. But it is only the introduction. It establishes the ground on which God as holy love acts in Christ.

Love in Action

The nature of love is to be totally open to the possibility of suffering, to be vulnerable to the other. And God in his will to create freely accepted the self-limitation of being rejected by his creature and of suffering the consequence of that rejection. It was not by any diktat or by force he could solve what Forsyth calls 'the grand problem of the restitution of the moral' and at the same time reconcile his rebellious creature to himself. That is not the way of love. That would not honour the freedom of the creature he loves.

The bridging of the gulf, atonement—to hang on to a biblical concept that still has value—must therefore have two principal and inter-related concerns; the vindication of God's moral reign, upholding of all his holiness demands and judging of evil, and the reconciliation and restitution of the creature he loves. From first to last, then, the atonement through the Cross and Resurrection of Christ is God's act alone. It is an action within the Godhead, accomplished at total cost to himself, a sacrifice freely accepted. But through the incarnation the sacrifice is made at a point in time within humanity, though in no way by a third party on behalf of humanity. And it is certainly not the placation of the Father by the Son. It is by God himself in the Son, who in the incarnation facing all manner of temptation, 'made fully like his brethren', yet remained without sin. The moral gulf was bridged by one fully God, fully man. To deny either would mean a defective bridge. As another theologian put it, 'The real objective element is that God made the atonement, and gave it finished to man'.[8] We stand on holy ground. We depend on the apostolic witness, for the Cross itself would have made little sense to us unless Jesus himself and then his first followers, guided by the promised Holy Spirit, had interpreted the event. Many who saw the crucifixion saw nothing but a bloody execution. Only through the kerygma of the Cross can we begin to enter its meaning.

Love Accepted

So, faced with God who is perfect in holiness, 'in whom is no darkness at all', and who in total self-giving establishes atonement through the Cross, man is at one and the same time brought low and lifted up, overwhelmed by unworthiness and joyfully restored with full pardon, declared morally bankrupt and enriched by grace. In the words of H. H. Farmer, in God at the Cross we are confronted by 'absolute demand and final succour'. It is in exploring that mystery we discover a window into divine love; indeed, more than that, we find ourselves embraced by that love and know ourselves to be reconciled and free. We begin to know in mind and heart and conscience something of the awesome mystery of what was done for us

> as Heaven's peace and perfect justice
> kissed a guilty world in love.

The Wondrous Cross

We must also take seriously another biblical theme, the wrath of God. His wrath is not to be understood as emotional antagonism towards creatures he has made, but as implacable opposition to the evil that takes them from his love, that ruins their fulfilment and robs them of the destiny for which they were created. And so God stops at nothing, not even the death on the Cross, to judge and put away the evil and its consequences.

There are without doubt different strands of understanding of the Cross, inter-related and cohering, within the totality of its benefits. Jesus, man of sorrows and acquainted with grief, bears our suffering, accepts all the evil we can project in insults, injustice and cruelty, enters into the depths of loneliness and rejection, and experiences death for us without complaint or bitterness. Jesus, through the naked power of sacrificial love, conquers the forces of hell and robs death of its sting as he rises to endless life. Jesus demonstrates that full acceptance is offered to all whatever they have done, whatever they are like, if only they come in the spirit that says,

> nothing in my hand I bring,
> simply to thy cross I cling.

Jesus at the Cross proves that nothing in all the universe shall be able to separate us from the love of God that is in him. But I am persuaded it is essential to emphasise that at its heart the atonement is something God had to do principally for his own sake as holy love. Though enacted in time at a particular moment and place, from eternity the Cross was in the heart of God. In creating the universe in love, with the possibility of rejection of his moral reign over all came the necessity of paying the price. Thus the Cross says, first of all, let God be God. His glory, his holiness, his reign of love matters most, but the glorious news for us is that in his self-vindication as God we are reconciled, redeemed, restored. Whether there are beings made in his image in other parts of the universe who likewise need reconciliation or not, for our own race the atonement is established complete. And so all who have come to share in it can join with Charles Wesley in confessing,

> Amazing love! How can it be
> that thou, my God, shouldst die for me?

The Word for All

To convey by word and deed the knowledge of this love of God is what evangelism is all about. The Christian Church cannot be what its Lord called it into being for unless it takes all opportunities to proclaim the Good News. No peoples are excluded from the right to hear it, for what God has done is for the whole of humanity. While it would be counter-productive, and indeed contrary to the way God himself comes to human beings, to give any groups, particularly of other faiths, the impression that they are being made targets in the Decade of Evangelism, it would be faithless to the Church's commission from its risen Lord to 'lay off' any peoples. All have to be treated with the respect God shows towards us his creatures. Their cherished beliefs and value-systems need to be understood, mutual trust established, and witness to God's love in Christ offered with sensitivity and the love that desires the highest good of the other, always recognising that God's Spirit may give us deeper understanding of truth through the encounter.

A Word for the Faithful

The Eucharist is at the centre of Anglican worship. Both the Catholic and Evangelical understandings of Eucharistic theology are anchored firmly in the Cross. It is from the finished work of atonement that saving benefits flow to the believing recipient within the koinonia of the Church. The sacrament declares a salvation objectively established and offered. But a full celebration of the Eucharist demands word and sacrament, kerygma and action. We like to think we maintain the balance of word and sacrament; in practice we often fall short. Sacramental actions may be given careful, even elaborate attention, while the exposition of the word can often appear to be of secondary importance, if the quality and time given to it are any criteria. This is not to argue, of course, for every sermon to be on the Cross; the full range of Christian teaching has to be covered. It is to plead for a new emphasis on the Cross, its centrality and meaning, in regular preaching, so that worshippers may see in and through the sacramental expressions the truth of what God has done for them, is doing and will do, and thus grow out of ill-informed, vague and even superstitious perceptions. There is no greater incentive to share the gospel of God's grace than a growing understanding of what it means to be able to say, 'The Son of God loved me and gave himself for me' (Galatians 2.20).

A Word of Testimony

In conclusion I want to speak personally of the privilege of being able to point men and women to the love of God in Christ crucified and risen. For over 40 years now I have been fully engaged in the ministry of a local parish. Other opportunities for service have come along in diocesan, national and Anglican Communion structures, but I remain basically a local minister of word and sacrament and pastor. And that involves being in constant relationship with the life-situations of a wide range of persons, as every pastor knows. There are couples facing a new life together in marriage and genuinely seeking God's help, or rejoicing at the wonder of a child entrusted to them and wanting God's blessing on the infant, even if very hazy as to what baptism is all about. Apparently without much warning a marriage splits apart and one of the partners at least is devastated. In another family cancer is diagnosed and weeks or months of agonizing anxiety overshadow the home. Suddenly a tragic accident strikes down a life in its prime, and a visit to the shocked, numbed relatives must be made. And every time the funeral director rings to arrange the service and committal there is a new grief situation to minister in, in some respects like every other, but each having its unique character and needs. Life causes one person to pass through a valley of doubt, faith in God is draining away, and yet there is a lingering desire to hang on. Another is overwhelmed with a sense of guilt, real or false, which lies beneath other emotional or physical manifestations.

In such critical moments of life, some of which come to all families at one time or other, the aspect of mission which is needed above all others is the telling of God's love in Christ in terms that relate to the situation that is dominating mind and heart. It is in a one to one relationship between the person and God that comfort, pardon, healing, strength to continue can come home. There is no greater privilege than being an agent under God in the creation of that relationship.

The proclamation of the Good News of God's reconciling love in Christ is, of course, not confined to crisis situations. In teaching and preaching the word takes root in persons of all ages by the operation of the Holy Spirit. The seed grows silently and the harvest is seen in Christ-like formation, sometimes in most unlikely lives. To see someone deeply committed in service for Christ, giving sacrificially, living close to God in prayer, looking for opportunities to speak of his love, is to be assured of the persuasive power of the word of the Cross. Can we doubt that the Suffering Servant 'sees the travail of his soul and is satisfied'? May God use his people in the Decade to bring multitudes to know in their lives his reconciling love in Christ and to go on to share it in turn with others.

Notes

1. *The Truth Shall Make You Free: The Lambeth Conference* 1988, ACC. Church House Publishing, pp. 32-5.
2. Ibid., p. 35.
3. ACC-3 Trinidad 1976, Report, p. 51.

4. *The Time is Now*, ACC-1, 1971, p. 42.
5. *Bonds of Affection*, ACC-6, 1984, p. 49.
6. *Anglicanism and the Universal Church*, Anglican Book Centre, Toronto, 1990, p. 290.
7. *The Gospel and Authority*, P. T. Forsyth, ed. M. Anderson, 1971.
8. A. M. Hunter in *P. T. Forsyth—Per Crucem ad Lucem*, 1974, p. 62.

Section I
Evangelism in Mission:
Everything Connects

1

PROCLAMATION OF GOOD NEWS

Essential Relationships of Mission and Evangelism

David Winter

Hearing and passing on news is part of the fuel of human satisfaction. Whether it is gossip between neighbours or the rather more sophisticated dissemination of news by the mass media, we want to be part of the process. We like to know the news and we enjoy passing it on. It is usually with genuine disappointment that someone says, 'And I was the last person to know about it'.

This is true of good news (the birth of a baby or an examination passed) or of bad news (illness, death or defeat in battle). No one wants to be the last to know. Of all the creatures on this planet, none is so distinctively communicative as *homo sapiens*. We have an insatiable appetite for information and an insatiable desire to pass it on.

Our most distinctive feature, in the world of the animals, is not our ability to walk on our hind legs or fashion artefacts with our hands, but to *speak*. It is through words that we have mastered our environment, ordered our society and enriched it with poetry, story and song. Others may express love. Only human beings can say 'I love you'. Others may be able to reason, but only humankind, with this priceless gift of language, can hold these ideas and concepts in our brains and then refine and develop them in recollection.

We are communicators, made in the image of a God who speaks. In the majestic account of creation in Genesis it is by *words* that he calls the universe into being: he spoke, and it was done. And in the unfolding history of Israel we find a God who speaks to his people, who reveals his name to Moses, who 'speaks through the prophets'. Finally, when God sent his Son into the world he was the *logos*, the Word: God's self-expression in human form. In him, communication was revealed in its perfection:

'God, who in the past spoke to our fathers through the prophets at many times and in various ways has in these last days spoken to us by his Son' (Heb. 1.1).

So it is consistent with what we know about ourselves and what we understand about God that the record of that unique act of communication through his Son is called 'good news', the Gospel. That story is the Church's most precious possession, given to us, like all news, in order to be passed on. It is now, and has always been, the Church's primary and essential task to make that good news known, and through it to build a new community based on its values.

Each of the four Gospels, in its own way, concludes with a command to the apostolic Church to engage itself in the continuing task of passing on the good news. They make it plain that the good news, far from being withdrawn, is now to be made universally available. Christ's followers, when endued with the Holy Spirit, would be the first agents of this extension.

In *Mark* the commission is stark in its simplicity: 'Go into all the world and preach the good news to all creation' (16.15). So speaks the 'epilogue' to the book whose first words heralded the 'beginning' of the good news. Now it is to continue, with cosmic dimensions: 'to all creation'.

In *Luke* the commission is, typically, to be 'witnesses'. This would be costly for the disciples. They might become 'martyrs' in the later sense of the word, giving their lives as a witness to the truth of the good news. But it would all be possible because of the gifts of the all-empowering Holy Spirit. In his strength, and *only* in his strength, the good news of Christ's suffering, death and resurrection, and of forgiveness through repentance and faith, will be proclaimed to 'all nations'. Of these truths they are the 'witnesses' (Luke 24.46ff).

In *Matthew* the commission picks up a prophecy of Daniel (7.14) that has run like a triumphant motif through the passion narrative: 'All authority in heaven and earth has been given to me. Therefore go and make disciples of all the nations . . .' In Christ's name his followers were to 'disciple' the nations, inviting them to gather around the divinely ordained Teacher and learn to obey everything he had commanded. They were to be baptised into a new community, where Jesus himself would be ever-present

4

('Surely I will be with you always, to the very end of the age'). Here is 'emmanuel' indeed (see Matt. 1.23)—'God with us'.

In the *Fourth Gospel*, as we might expect, the commission has a more interior quality. The risen Jesus came to his overjoyed disciples and said, 'As the Father has sent me, I am sending you'. He followed the words with an action, breathing on them and then saying, 'Receive the Holy Spirit. If you forgive anyone his sins, they are forgiven; if you do not forgive them, they are not forgiven' (John 20.21-3).

Their calling was to minister forgiveness in Christ's name and in the power of the Holy Spirit. The method by which they were to do this is both startlingly simple and devastatingly radical: 'As the Father has sent me, I am sending you'. The task, overwhelming in its scope as spelt out in the synoptic Gospels, is here put in an exemplary framework. They are to be sent out *in the same way* as the Father sent out Jesus. The pattern of their ministry, in other words, is to be nothing less than the incarnation itself.

That comparison determines the nature of the Church's subsequent mission. It is to be, in a real sense, an extension of the incarnation—not a repetition of it, nor a duplication of it, but an extension. The Father's purpose in sending his Son into the world is to be fulfilled by his Son's disciples. 'As the Father sent me, so I am sending you.' They are not sent out as *conquistadores*, to demand submission to their message, but—after the pattern of Jesus—as those who identify and share.

They will, as Jesus did, stand alongside people in their need. They will, as Jesus did, share the good news from God with the spiritually bankrupt ('the poor'). They will, as Jesus did, minister healing from within the circle of need, not from some vantage point outside it. They will, as Jesus did, enflesh the love of God in human circumstances. Mark, Matthew and Luke write the agenda. John, in the upper room, prescribes the method.

It is here, it seems to me, that the essential relationship of mission and evangelism is created. The whole Church is involved in 'mission', because we are a people who are 'sent'. The body of Christ (in Paul's vividly incarnational phrase) exists for the world, to extend his saving ministry to all people. That mission mirrors his own, a mission of message, miracle and meal. He spoke with authority and people listened. He touched lives with the power of God and they were made whole. He ate with

5

tax-gatherers and sinners and drew them to discipleship. He met the intellectual, spiritual and social needs of people by being with them, 'on their side' as we might say. That is what his Father sent him to do, and it is what our Lord himself sends us to do.

That is 'mission', meeting the total needs of humankind with the total love of God, along the entire interface between the community of faith and what the New Testament calls 'the world', human society organised as though God did not exist. Mission is all-embracing, as the ministry of Jesus was. It is words and loving action and caring relationship. It is justice and peace. It is healing and forgiveness. We are a mission people, because we are *sent*.

But within that total mission there is an essential element which concerns the proclamation of the 'good news' and this we properly call 'evangelism'. God sent Jesus to *be* the good news, it is true. All that he said and did, his life, his death and his resurrection, constitute the good news. It was, and always is, action before words. After all, the inarticulate baby of Bethlehem was described in the angelic message as 'good news'.

But the good news needs to be articulated, sooner or later. Jesus came into Galilee *proclaiming* the good news as well as *being* it. 'This good news of repentance and forgiveness of sins will be *preached* in his name to all nations' (Luke 24.47). Within the total mission of the Church, evangelism—the proclaiming or sharing of the good news about Jesus Christ—is an essential element. It cannot be an optional extra, nor can it be simply subsumed into all the other aspects of mission. If that happens, we betray part of the mission itself, for clearly, both in dominical command and apostolic example, the saving *message* must accompany the saving *ministry*. Of course, as we have seen, the gospel is action before it is words, but in the normal course of events it must eventually involve words, or it is a mission without meaning. First the action, then the explanation—that is the usual pattern of the ministry of Jesus and indeed that is the usual pattern of people's journey into faith. Mission is a way of life. Evangelism is making that way 'known'.

How could it be other for creatures who place so much value on words? It is true that we wish to be shown love. But it is an undeniable feature of human experience that we also need to be told that we are loved. God has shown us his love in Jesus. But

6

he also asks that the good news of that love should be 'proclaimed'. 'How beautiful are the feet of those who preach good
news'

> Evangelism is the making known of the gospel of the Lord Jesus
> Christ, especially to those who do not know it . . . We are charged to
> communicate that the life, death and resurrection of Jesus Christ is
> good news from God. Evangelism usually involves the use of words,
> but not inevitably so. Identification and solidarity with people are
> indispensable and may themselves be forms of evangelism if they
> evoke a response which enables Jesus Christ to be 'named'.[1]

That 'identification' and 'solidarity' which the Church of
England Board for Mission and Unity in that statement described
as 'indispensable' themselves speak of the principle of incarnation, which sets the disciple alongside and within human need.
But it is *in the name of Jesus Christ* that the disciple offers
forgiveness and healing. That 'name' must be made known. To
do less is to offer good news without reason, meaning or content.
To do other (and take the credit ourselves) verges on blasphemy.

Evangelism, then, is essential to the Church's mission. 'The
task of evangelising all peoples is the essential mission of the
Church,' wrote Pope Paul VI in his encyclical 'Evangelisation in
the Modern World'. 'Evangelism is the primary task given to the
Church', said the Lambeth Conference of 1988, in calling for a
Decade of Evangelism. Evangelising is of the essence of the
Church, of its very being, because without it the Church would
not exist. And it is primary, of first importance, because it is the
gospel, the *kerygma*, that brings the Church into being, and not
vice versa.

Despite this, evangelism has not had a good press in recent
decades. Many Christians associate it with proselytism, with
emotional pressure aimed at conversion, with strange people who
accost you in the street and enquire if you are 'saved'. Others
think of it solely in terms of what is called mass evangelism—
famous preachers with vast crowds in football stadia and a meeting
which inevitably ends in a call for an immediate response.

Now these may—or in some cases may not—be legitimate
means of evangelism. But evangelism itself is nothing more nor
less than the willingness of the Christian Church to share with

7

those who do not yet have them the riches of the good news about Jesus.

The opening chapter of Mark's Gospel describes this 'good news' as *from* God, *about* Jesus and *for* us (see Mark 1.14, 1.1, 1.17). At different times in the New Testament it is called the 'good news of God', 'the good news of Christ' and 'the good news of the kingdom'. The first describes its origin: God is its instigator. The second describes its method: God's intention or 'plan' was achieved through the coming of his Son. The third describes its results: those who repent and believe 'become 'kingdom' people, seeking to live together and in the world under God's gracious and generous rule.

To put it another way, the good news is 'of' or 'from' God—it is God's good news. It originates in his plan and purpose. It is good news 'about' Jesus Christ, his Son—it focuses on God's action in calling, anointing and sending Jesus on his mission. It is good news driven by the Holy Spirit: 'The Spirit sent him out . . .' (Mark 1.12). It is good news of the kingdom of God, whose time has come (Mark 1.15), the day when people can recognise his authority, justice and salvation and respond to them appropriately with changed wills ('repentance') and changed minds ('belief'). It is thoroughly trinitarian good news, which expresses the richness of the nature of God and speaks to the wholeness of human beings. And it centres on the action of God in the coming of Jesus.

In the teaching of Jesus as we find it in the synoptic Gospels, the central note is 'the good news of the kingdom'. He brought to the down-trodden people, the 'lost sheep of the house of Israel', news of a new kingdom of freedom, justice and righteousness, where the years of bitter subjugation to the rule of Greek and Roman Emperors would be replaced by the gracious and gentle rule of God. And he himself was the key to that kingdom.

To share this good news with others is, in New Testament language, to 'evangelise'. 'Evangelism'—a word which does not occur in the Bible—is simply an abstract noun developed from the verb. It is the process by which the good news is shared, rather than any specific way of doing it.

Incidentally, I would take the word 'evangelisation', which seems to be preferred in Roman Catholic circles, to describe the results of effective evangelism. When you have evangelised, when a person or community has been permeated with the truths and insights of the good news, then you have 'evangelisation'. Christians are people who have been evangelised. The Church is not only an evangelising community but one that has been evangelised. And that is not a once-for-all experience; as the good news takes root in us and among us, we go on being 'evangelised' by it. The process never ends short of the day when we shall know 'even as we are known'.

But to return to 'evangelism'. If it is, as I suggest, the process by which the good news is proclaimed, it is obviously important that those doing the 'proclaiming' are clear about the content of the message itself. Some research in England[2] suggests that a major reason why churches fail to evangelise is a lack of confidence about that message. It is not that they do not believe it for themselves, but that they feel uninformed and ill-equipped to expose their own beliefs to the searching wind of secular scrutiny. There is also often a feeling that Christians themselves are not agreed about the content of the good news.

In fact their fears may be groundless. During 1990 I asked some forty different gatherings of Christians in the Oxford diocese, some clergy, some laity and some mixed, to attempt, in small groups of five or six, to summarise the Christian good news in not more than twenty-five words. I suppose some fifteen hundred people would have been involved, across the entire spectrum of Anglican traditions, catholic, evangelical, liberal and charismatic.

There was an astonishing degree of unanimity. Almost without exception (and certainly without prompting) groups opted to focus their summaries on the action of God in Jesus. From the replies I kept, it is possible to draw up a kind of consensus summary, as follows: 'God loves us, sent his Son Jesus to die for us and raised him from death. Those who trust in him receive forgiveness and new life'. Obviously that is not a full statement of the *kerygma*. It does not say that Christ died for our sins. It does not mention the work of the Holy Spirit. It omits the call to repentance. And, significantly perhaps, it is highly individualistic: the concept of the kingdom and of the cosmic and universal dimension of

Christianity is absent. Yet in so far as it is possible in twenty-five words it does capture, I believe, the heart of the message of the New Testament, and a summary of that kind drew almost unanimous support.

Differences and difficulties tended to arise if more precise definitions were sought: a problem not unknown to compilers of credal statements throughout church history. But while the groups kept to God's saving actions through Jesus there was clearly common ground, and that common ground is essentially the *kerygma* itself. Incidentally, the consensus summary is not all that far away from the twenty-five word statement that gave me the idea for the whole exercise: 'God so loved the world that he gave his one and only Son, that whoever believes in him should not perish but have eternal life' (John 3.16).

Of course this is not all there is to know about the good news, much less is it all there is to know about the Christian faith. The gospel itself includes a sharp moral dimension (see e.g. Luke 18.22), an insistent call to a new way of life ('repentance') and a commitment to discipleship within the body of Christ ('baptism'). But if the apostolic Church baptised upon profession of Jesus as Lord, as we presume from the biblical evidence (see e.g. 1 Cor. 12.3), there seems little ground for making the initial message today unduly complicated. After all, the *kerygma* was to be followed by the *didache*, the decision by discipleship; and it still is.

Evangelism itself must be about a message, however it is transmitted. Christians believe that message has within itself enormous potential. For Jesus, the good seed of the gospel produced fruit, multiplying over and over again. His 'words' give life (John 6.63); they are a foundation for living (Matt. 7.24); they minister not only forgiveness but moral transformation (John 8.11). Where the seed of the good news is faithfully sown and carefully nurtured, the harvest should be kingdom values, kingdom life-style and kingdom justice.

That is why evangelism and mission are indivisible. Without evangelism mission is incomplete; without mission evangelism is impoverished. The world cannot be changed and its unjust systems reformed unless people are changed and re-formed by the good news of the kingdom. 'Unjust systems' cannot repent: only morally autonomous human beings can do that.

But people will not believe the *words* of the good news and repent if they do not see in the gospel community, the Church, their promised fruit. Mission without evangelism lacks a cutting edge. Evangelism without mission lacks credibility.

It would be encouraging if the Decade of Evangelism could signal a moratorium to the arid squabble between those who think evangelism should take priority over mission and those who think mission should take priority over evangelism. The first case is often put this way: 'People's souls are more important than their bodies, eternal issues than political or social ones, so let us concentrate on bringing men and women to salvation in Christ. If we do the task well, eventually, by a trickle-down process, society itself will be transformed.' The contrary case is sometimes put in this way: 'While injustice, inequality and deprivation blight the lives of people, they cannot hear the good news. When we have grappled seriously with these issues as Christians, *then* will be the time to tell them about Jesus and eternal life.'

Of course, those summaries have elements of caricature in them, but both attitudes, in something like those terms, are constantly encountered in the Church. The argument I am proposing is that it is not a case of *either* evangelism *or* mission, but of both as complementary elements in the life of the Church. Mission includes evangelism and should not neglect it. Evangelism cannot exist healthily apart from mission, and should not strive for a reckless independence from it. They are not identical (though Christians often and wrongly use the words as synonyms) but they are interdependent.

As part of its preparation for the Decade of Evangelism the Oxford diocese in England carried out a research project on church growth. The advisory group on mission consulted the archdeacons of the three counties in the diocese in order to draw up a list of 'growing' churches. These were churches where the congregation was genuinely growing, bringing people to faith in Christ or back to the practice of a faith they had neglected, by conversion, nurture, teaching or pastoral care. They were not churches that had grown by transfer or through population growth in the parish.

From visits to these parishes an interesting report was compiled. From it the group identified a list of criteria common to all of the fourteen churches researched—criteria which seemed

11

to be present where churches were growing. They were, in some ways, rather surprising.

1 Care for the needy within the congregation.
2 Structures (e.g. small groups) for the open sharing of faith by members of the congregation.
3 The ability to manage change within the church.
4 A collaborative style of leadership.
5 Evidence of prayer life.
6 Good giving of money.
7 Lively, varied and sincere worship.
8 A concern for, and action within, the locality.
9 The setting of clear and realisable objectives and regular reviews of parish strategy.
10 The sense that the laity is to be the church in the world and not just clerical helpers within the congregation (i.e. an outward-looking rather than an inward-looking attitude).

It has to be stressed that these were churches which were genuinely growing, bringing people to a living faith. In other words, they were churches where evangelism was not just talked about, but happening. And yet they were also seen to be churches which 'care for the needy', were 'concerned and active in the locality' and were 'outward-looking'. If we put those characteristics alongside a life of prayer, worship and fellowship we have a picture not unlike that Luke offers us of the embryonic church in Jerusalem (Acts 2.41ff), where prayer, teaching, fellowship and eucharist were matched by the sharing of possessions and loving care for the needy. Now, as then, evangelism could not be divorced from mission. Sharing the good news of Christ and living in the world by its demanding standards are not conflicting aims for the Church but two aspects of the same one.

The Anglican Primates have expressed this position of interdependence in powerful and emotive language:

In a Decade of Evangelism we seek for a moment to lift up this great act of proclamation, properly called evangelism, which holds out to women and men everywhere the person of Jesus Christ. As people in the power of the Holy Spirit are drawn to him, so are they drawn to God, to one another and to all creation. On this sure foundation may be built all our ministries of love.[3]

It is on this 'sure foundation', what St Paul calls the 'only foundation, Jesus Christ' (1 Cor. 3.11), that we may build the vocation to evangelise into the fabric of the total mission of the Church. If we succeed, our evangelism will be credible and our mission comprehensive. If we fail, we shall quite simply have failed God and the gospel.

Notes

1. Board for Mission and Unity, Partnership for World Mission 1987 p. 38.
2. Oxford Diocesan Visitation returns 1989.
3. In their Cyprus 'Guidelines for the Decade' 1989.

2

DECADE OF TRANSFORMATION

Proclaiming, Celebrating and Following Christ
as the Paradigm of Change in People,
Church and Society

Janet Hodgson

Amada en el Amado transformada. (The lover, i.e. the soul, is transformed into her beloved, i.e. God.)   *St John of the Cross*

Preamble

Recently a group of Church of England clergy were asked to
select a word describing what the Christian faith meant to them.
A surprising number chose the word transformation.[1] In the
last ten years transformation has increasingly become a key word
in inter-Anglican discussions around the world. This represents
a major paradigm shift from an exclusively other-worldly, tran-
scendental and individualistic understanding of salvation to one
that is holistic and corporate, touching the whole person and
embracing the socio-political dimension of society as well as the
environment. The new awareness in the worldwide Church,
which recognises transformation as the true essence of Christian
salvation, has been dearly won through the Christian witness of
poor and oppressed peoples in the southern hemisphere throughout their liberation struggle. Transformation has social, political
and economic implications. A true understanding of transformation under the aegis of the Church can only happen by taking
seriously the context of the Church in the Third World. The
Church in the First World cannot set the agenda. We must guard
against the debate on mission and evangelism being hijacked by
theologians in the west.

The term transformation first came into vogue in Anglican
circles at the Anglican Consultative Council (ACC-6) meeting in
Badagry, Nigeria, in 1984, ousting the term development to

describe Christian social responsibility. ACC-6 followed the International Evangelical Consultation on the Nature and Mission of the Church (Wheaton, Ill., 1983) in defining transformation as:

a change from a level of human existence that is less than that envisaged by our Creator, to one in which man (*sic*) is fully human and free to move to a state of wholeness in harmony with God, with fellow human beings and with every aspect of his (*sic*) environment.[2]

'Development' had become discredited because of the implication that some countries had reached a higher stage of development than others and needed no further change. ACC-6 stood by the radical notion that transformation involved material as well as spiritual change and that this would impact upon the haves and the have-nots quite differently:

The so-called 'developed world' needs transformation to free itself from a secular, materialistic condition marked by broken relationships, violence, economic subjugation, and devastation of nature. And the under-developed world needs transformation from the subhuman condition of poverty, premature death, oppression, disease, ignorance and superstition.[3]

ACC-6 defined one of the four marks of mission as being 'to seek to transform the unjust structures of society'. This was reaffirmed by the Lambeth Conference of 1988, the Primates' Meeting in Cyprus in 1989, and the ACC-8 meeting in Wales in 1990. The bishops at the 1988 Lambeth Conference spelt out the social and political consequences of taking a theology of transformation seriously in no uncertain terms:

Transformation of structures will often involve political action. Transformation will mean that all that demeans human dignity (e.g. discrimination on grounds of race, sex or class), or prevents proper access to basic community resources (e.g. medical and educational facilities), or pollutes the environment or allows natural resources to be plundered (e.g. the removal of fish by some powers in the Pacific Ocean or the removal of indigenous people from their land) is to be resisted.[4]

The 1988 Lambeth Conference issued a pastoral letter entitled 'On the Gospel and transformation' in which transformation was seen as the theological linchpin which holds inner personal change and socio-political change firmly together 'in one Gospel and one witness in the one Body.'[5] ACC-8 took up the challenge in stressing that this concept of transformation can be a corrective to any tendency to isolate evangelism from social responsibility. 'The Decade of Evangelism must also be a decade of transformation', they said, and this premise underscored their debate:

> The definition of mission, whether in the broader context of the Church's prophetic role ... or in the more specialised area of evangelism, ... inevitably involves the prospect of change, not only in the unjust structures of society but in the Church itself, in individual Christians and in those to whom the good news is made known. Transformation is implied in any consideration of justice in a world where injustice is widely manifest.[6]

Jesus' Truth

When Pontius Pilate confronted Jesus in the Praetorium with the question, 'What is truth?', our Lord made no answer. Instead, he went on to be lifted up on the Cross, to usher in God's kingdom, a new heaven and a new earth, a new creation, a new Adam, and a new covenant. But why did our Lord miss out on this splendid opportunity to evangelise Pilate, whose query about truth, however flippant or mocking, surely seemed to open a door to an altar call?

Jesus' truth, unlike the truth of the philosophers of Athens and the hot-gospellers of today, is the truth of the flesh. It can only be experienced and transmitted through the crucible of praxis. This experience is more than just a feeling of being 'strangely warmed within'. It is nothing less than the total transformation, in body, mind and spirit, of people, not as isolated individuals but as members of a transfigured, liberated and healed community. In the words of South African theologian, John de Gruchy:

> From the perspective of the kingdom of God personal and social transformation belong together and it is totally false and unbiblical to suggest that they can be separated. God's will and purpose is not only the transformation of our own lives and relationships but also the transformation and renewal of society.[7]

16

To preach Jesus' truth is not just to cry 'Lord, Lord', but to do the will of the heavenly Father (Matt. 7.21-23). Evangelism is an incarnational event. Preaching the good news is no mere verbal gesture. It amounts to making the good news happen. Our Lord himself defines bringing the good news as proclaiming liberty to the captives, restoring sight to the blind, letting the oppressed go free, and announcing the Jubilee year, which signals the restoration of all that has been taken away from the dispossessed (Luke 4.18-19). It has been the Third World Christians' contribution to contemporary theology to insist that at the heart of the Christian *kerygma* is the coming of the Reign of God. In *The Road to Damascus* (1989), Christians from seven nations— South Africa, Namibia, South Korea, the Philippines, El Salvador, Nicaragua and Guatemala—witness:

> The Reign of God is not simply a way of speaking about the next world. The Reign of God is this world completely transformed in accordance with God's plan. It is like the Jubilee year of Leviticus 25 when all those who are living in slavery will be set free, when all debts will be cancelled and when the land will be restored to those from whom it was stolen. The Reign of God begins in this life but stretches out beyond this life. It is transcendent and eschatological without being unconcerned about the problems and suffering of the poor in this life.[8]

Hundreds of people from diverse Church traditions in the seven different countries were involved in the preparation of *The Road to Damascus* over two and a half years, and it was signed by thousands more. Their concern was to lay bare the historical roots of polarisation among Christians in their own countries. Subtitled 'Kairos and Conversion', their document seeks to affirm the faith of the poor and the oppressed, to condemn the sin of those who exploit, persecute and kill people, and to call to conversion those who take the name of the Lord but have strayed from Jesus' truth.

The Heresy of Evangelism as Conformation

Too often the traditional Church of western Christendom has restricted evangelism to the transmission of a set of articles of faith to be heard and received without any commitment or sense of urgency to incarnate the faith in the reality of injustice and suffering. The gospel is reduced to little more than the saving of souls, the emphasis being on a change of heart, remorse and a 'spiritual' regeneration. Sin is understood in narrowly moralistic and individualistic terms: swearing, alcoholism, theft, fornication, adultery, murder, and the like. Salvation is seen as exclusively private, fulfilling the need to be absolved from individual guilt. Proclamation becomes a call for a subjective, interior, 'spiritual', privatised conversion without reference to the incarnational and corporate dimension of sin. Jesus' truth is thus divorced from the reality of the world, which remains unchallenged, untouched and unaltered. The good news of the white western Church has all too often become bad news for the poor. The Roman Catholic theologian, Albert Nolan, writes:

> It was the 'spiritualisation' and privatisation of religion that enabled the system of exploitation and colonialism to be justified, enabled to expand through the world and cause the most barbaric excess of suffering in the history of humankind. This kind of religion is, without doubt, the opium of the people.[9]

In South Africa a group of evangelical theologians identified as 'Concerned Evangelicals' has protested how traditional evangelism has allowed so-called Christians in the apartheid system to lead pietistic lives and still oppress, exploit and dehumanize people. Their victims are dissuaded from complaining or resisting because this would be tantamount to worrying about 'earthly' concerns that supposedly had nothing to do with Christian spirituality. Thus blacks have been coerced into focusing on 'heavenly' things no matter that fellow white Christians were dispossessing them of their land and God-ordained humanity.[10]

Even with winds of change blowing through South Africa, after a temporary honeymoon with the struggle for transformation, there is always the danger of the Church's 'return to the sanctuary'. Many Christians have backed off from political involvement since the new dispensation in February 1990. The weakness of the prophetic tradition within the South African Church makes it particularly vulnerable to being co-opted into legitimising the conformist theology of the state.[11]

The insidious heresy of evangelism as conformation probably has its roots in an exaggeration of the Reformation doctrine of imputed righteousness, which posited the saved Christian person as at once righteous and sinful (*simul justus et peccator*). The Fathers of the Reformation, Luther, Calvin and Zwingli, could hardly have foreseen how Christian salvation in Protestant circles would later come to mean sinful persons and sinful structures being justified, i.e. pardoned, but in no way sanctified, i.e. transformed. This legalistic distortion of the doctrine of imputed nature of grace and salvation has somehow coloured the Church's vision of evangelism. The sinful social structures which created and perpetuated suffering, poverty and oppression were not themselves regarded as things to be saved, converted or transformed. Conventional evangelism became obsessed with saving and converting the soul. As Nolan says:

> The gospel is about salvation from sin. But it is more than my personal salvation from my personal sins, no matter how important that is. The salvation which Jesus promised was the coming of God's kingdom . . . Whatever else the word 'kingdom' may mean, it was in Jesus' time the word for a nation or society. Jesus was talking about a community. Salvation meant a new community, a new society, a new universal nation: the kingdom of God. And this is where social justice comes in. Work for social justice is part of God's work of saving the world. It is not separate from salvation, not an optional extra. It is that part of God's saving work which is redeeming unjust structures, saving societies . . . We must convert individuals, but we must also try to change structures. They are all part of God's saving work . . .
>
> If we are going to be effective evangelists, one of the first things we're going to have to do in our preaching is to recover the pervasiveness of sin, and the fact that sin is something that goes far beyond my soul.[12]

The perennial dichotomy between proclamation and praxis is possibly the most cancerous heresy that has plagued the Body of Christ and kept Jesus' truth from touching and transforming the very world for which he laid down his life. The liberating theology of Third World Christians has finally set out to nail this heresy of conformation to the status quo. Taking Jesus himself as the role model, they regard evangelism as participation in the process of conversion of social structures which hold them captive. To evangelise is to challenge the status quo. To preach

Christ is to put on Christ. To proclaim Jesus' truth is to practise it. Archbishop George Carey was echoing this sense of urgency when he said that 'living the gospel . . . is a true expression of an evangelising and missionising Church.'[13] This close identification of evangelism with liberation is also reflected in Pope Paul VI's encyclical entitled *On the Evangelization of Peoples* (1975):

> The church has the duty to proclaim the liberation of millions of human beings, many of whom are its own children—the duty of assisting the birth of this liberation, of giving witness to it, of ensuring that it is complete. This is not foreign to evangelization.[14]

Here for the first time the term 'liberation' in its political sense became enshrined in official papal teaching.

Critique of State Theology

The worldwide Church is commemorating 1992 as the five-hundredth anniversary of Christopher Columbus' 'discovery' of America and the launch of Europe's grand era of mission and evangelism. For the west it is an occasion to celebrate the extension of white Christendom into the 'new world'. For native people, however, it signals the beginning of the end of their God-ordained spiritual identity inherited from an ancient tradition. The mission theology of the invading Euro-culture into which indigenous people were assimilated is assessed by *The Road to Damascus* theologians:

> The God whom the missionaries preached was a God who blessed the powerful, the conquerors, the colonisers. This God demanded resignation in the face of oppression and condemned rebelliousness and insubordination. All that was offered to us by this God was an interior and other-worldly liberation. It was a God who dwelt in heaven and in the Temple but not in the world.
>
> The Jesus who was preached to us was barely human. He seemed to float above history, above all human problems and conflicts. He was pictured as a high and mighty king or emperor who ruled over us, even during his earthly life, from the heights of his majestic throne. His approach to the poor was therefore thought of as condescending. He condescended to make the poor the objects of his mercy and compassion without sharing their oppression and their struggles. His

20

death had nothing to do with historical conflicts, but was a human sacrifice to placate an angry God. What was preached to us was a completely other-worldly Jesus who had no relevance to this life.[15]

Following an other-worldly Jesus holds the temptation to be conformed to the world as it is instead of seeking to transform it and so become transformed oneself (cf. Rom. 12.2). Third World theologians have exposed the persistent bias of the traditional Church to conform to the norms and values of the society of its time even when they conflict with Jesus' truth. In South Africa escalating violence in the mid-1980s challenged the Churches there to emerge from the complacency of their religious ghettoes and question their relevance in the crisis situation. With the townships going up in flames, thousands imprisoned, missing, or fleeing for their lives, and a national state of emergency declared, Christians from different denominations, lay and ordained, came together to reflect theologically and wrestle with the Church's role in this context. As a result *The Kairos Document* was drafted in September 1985.

The unprecedented level of state repression and the sacrificial cost of people's resistance was recognised as the time of truth, as the new *kairos*, 'the moment of grace and opportunity . . . in which God issues a challenge to decisive action.'[16] *The Kairos Document* pitted God's challenge to transformative action against the state's claim to be divinely ordained and so justify the status quo with its racism, capitalism and totalitarianism. This godless State Theology was seen to bless injustice, canonise the will of the powerful, reduce the poor to blind obedience, all this by co-opting theological concepts and biblical texts to service its own reactionary agenda. The Kairos theologians revealed how in the past even the more liberal Churches were co-opted by the state to give it tacit support. The Church was found guilty of replacing Jesus' truth with the heresy of State Theology.

Inspired by the Kairos debate, the 'Concerned Evangelicals' met in 1985 to make a critique of their own theology and practice. This appeared as *Evangelical Witness in South Africa* the following year.[17] The word 'evangelical' was broadly defined to include Christians who belonged to the charismatic and pentecostal churches. A group of 'concerned pentecostals' also felt the need to confess their specific complicity in upholding State Theology and produced *A Relevant Pentecostal Witness* in 1988. They warned that

> a Pentecostalism [or any form of right-wing religion] that ignores the concrete situation in which it works, can be extremely dangerous in its irrelevance. It can easily be infiltrated and manipulated by racist ideologies and exploitative structures.[18]

When the Church becomes the handmaid of the state how can she incarnate the mind of Christ?

Transformation of the Church

The Church is the chosen community entrusted with the vocation to heal and redeem the wounded world. The Church which becomes 'the leaven of the Pharisees' (Matt.16.11) can transform nothing. Third World Christians have opened our eyes to see how the Church itself has become a site of struggle between the oppressor and the oppressed, who both appropriate the gospel to seek religious legitimation for their respective stands. It is in the interest of reactionary forces to leave the Church ever trapped into servicing their exploitative ideology. The calling of the progressive forces, however, is to help transform the Church itself so that it may become like the parabolic leaven 'which a woman took and hid in three measures of flour until it was all leavened' (cf. Matt 13.33).

CASE STUDY I: SOUTH AFRICA

Reform experienced in countries like South Africa is treated with great suspicion because sinful social structures are in principle irreformable. Any reform would be calculated not to serve the common good but rather to preserve the interests of the minority from whom it received its mandate. In the words of Albert Nolan, reform in South Africa is

> the new way of gaining some measure of legitimacy for the same old system and of conditioning people to accept the new security measures. It is a further extension of the old policy of co-option . . . More and more efforts will be made to win the minds and hearts of the people and to restructure the system . . . But such reforms cannot

work because they always come from the top, are designed to benefit the ruling class and will never allow the people as a whole to participate fully ... The system cannot change itself to become something quite different. The system can only adapt itself in order to remain fundamentally the same. All its reforms are simply ways of self-adaptation that can only lead to more contradictions, more crises, more conflict and more chaos.[19]

The South African Government has indeed scrapped some of the racist laws to make way for the lifting of sanctions but land has yet to be restored to black people and structures supporting the social and economic privileges of the white minority remain intact. As Archbishop Desmond Tutu says, 'the reforms are like the curate's egg, good in parts; falling much short of the radical changes which the people want and need'.[20] What they are looking for is 'justice from below', which is the way forward for the Church in South Africa.

In order to be renewed the Church must constantly analyse the signs of our times. As the Kairos theologians argue, it can no more rely upon a few stock ideas derived from the liberal Christian tradition (such as peace, non-violence, reconciliation, love) and seek to apply them *a priori* to an impenitent situation.[21] There can be no true peace and no true reconciliation without justice. The Church has to heed the prophetic admonition and not cry 'peace' where there is no real peace (Jer. 6.14; Ezek. 13.10). It should not be tempted to follow the path of neutral mediation and persuade those who are oppressed to accept oppression for the sake of peace. For too long the reformist-conformist Church in South Africa and elsewhere has preached a God who will intervene in his own good time to put right what is wrong in the world. That leaves very little for human beings to do except pray for God's intervention. In order that it may be a truly transformed body representative of the spirit of the new South Africa, the Church must proclaim a God who sides with the poor, and calls his Church to pray for the kingdom, not by waiting upon God's intervention, but by actively mobilising and empowering people to incarnate his will in the corporate witness of the Christian community.

To its credit one may say that through the courageous witness of its leaders the Church in South Africa has become a sacrament

23

of resistance. It has brought forth a whole new hermeneutics of struggle, looking at the Scripture from the perspective of the township and Robben Island. Archbishop Tutu voiced the Church's protest to State theology when he confessed, 'I am puzzled about which Bible people are reading when they suggest religion and politics don't mix.'

In November 1990 the urgent need for Christians in South Africa to forge a united witness to meet the challenge of a rapidly changing political situation brought together 230 leaders from 97 different Church denominations and 40 Church-related organisations at Rustenburg in the Transvaal. They drafted *The Rustenburg Declaration*, which unequivocally denounces apartheid as sin and makes a clear confession of guilt, the whites for their complicity in either practising or failing to resist apartheid, and the victims for acquiescing in their oppression. Moreover, the Declaration underscores the need to see Christian forgiveness in terms of transformation: 'confession and forgiveness necessarily require restitution. Without it, a confession of guilt is incomplete.'[23]

CASE STUDY II: NATIVE PEOPLE IN THE CANADIAN CHURCH

In 1985 a Native American woman from a salmon-fishing community on a small island in British Columbia called upon the United Church of Canada to make an apology for stripping her people of their native spiritual identity in the name of mission for Christ. The following year Moderator Robert Smith made history by leading his Church in making a formal Act of Apology to their native congregations at the United Church's General Council meeting in Sudbury:

> Long before my people journeyed to this land your people were here, and you received from your elders an understanding of creation, and of the mystery that surrounds us all, that was deep and rich and to be treasured. We did not hear you when you shared your vision. In our zeal to tell you of the good news of Jesus Christ we were closed to the value of your spirituality. We confused western ways and culture with the depth and breadth and length and height of the gospel of Jesus Christ. We imposed our civilization as a condition of accepting the gospel. We tried to make you be like us and in so doing

24

we helped to destroy the vision that made you what you were. As a result you, and we, are poorer and the image of the Creator is twisted, blurred and we are not what we are meant by God to be. We ask you to forgive us and to walk together with us in the spirit of Christ so that our peoples may be blessed and God's creation healed.[24]

The Apology is a very positive way for the Canadian Church to initiate the process of self-renewal. But it is just the beginning. Confession of colonial sin in itself will not bring in Christ's kingdom unless, as in South Africa, there is also a move towards restoration and reparation of the damage done. A truly transformed Church will not content itself with an apology for its complicity in colonialism but will follow it up with a full-scale campaign for 'political forgiveness', i.e. forgiveness that results in the healing of social structures which have crippled Native Canadians.

A Church which evangelises in the name of a God who emptied himself of all power must seek to empower the powerless by calling for a radical change in the balance of power between the white Canadians and the First People of the continent. Otherwise, even after restoration of land and other rights, Native people will continue to be vulnerable to exploitation. Empowering Native people should be the top priority on the agenda of the Canadian Church during the Decade of Evangelism. Short of this political vision evangelism would be bad news for the poor. No wonder the Diocese of the Arctic in the Anglican Church of Canada has expressed strong reservations about the Decade. For them, historically, evangelism has gone hand in hand with the plundering of their natural resources and 'cultural, spiritual and racial genocide'.[25]

Christ: The Paradigm of Transformation

Transformation becomes the crux of evangelism not because the Church needs to update and modernise her image in accordance with the current secular issues such as development, justice, liberation, integrity of creation, etc. To see evangelism as transformation is the most radical way of living up to the vocation of the Church of Christ because it takes us to the very root of Christian evangelism, i.e. the person of Christ himself.

Evangelism today must once again grapple with the prime question of theology: who is Jesus Christ?

In Christ the eternal Word of God became flesh. Christ is thus the archaic and cosmic mode of all becoming, all change, all healing, all liberation. He is the first fruits of God's new creation. The patristic doctrine of the incarnation speaks of ordinary flesh becoming divine flesh, flesh being sanctified by the spirit of God. When the incarnate Christ took residence in the world, he initiated the process of transformation of our humanity, of the entire created order including our human societies with their myriad structures. The Divine descended into the world so that the world could grow into the Divine. Christ did not come to redeem souls *out* of the unredeemable world but to redeem them *into* a redeemed world.

Proclaiming Christ as Saviour without spelling out the nature of sin permeating the structures of the old order, is evangelism in a vacuum. It is a mere ejaculation of an unlived-out faith which has no point of reference to the alienation and oppression in the concrete world of flesh and matter. When John the Baptist sent messengers to ask Jesus if he was the promised Messiah, our Lord did not glibly answer the question in the affirmative. Instead, he recited the kingdom values that were taking shape in the faith community around him. He sent the messengers back to John with the message, 'Go and tell John what you have seen and heard: how the blind recover their sight, the lame walk, the lepers are made clean, the deaf hear, the dead are raised to life, the poor are hearing the good news' (Luke 7.22-23).

There is thus total unity between the Messiah and the Messianic kingdom; so also there is total unity between the preached word and the transformation and new creation that must necessarily follow. The understanding of the Word as the creative and transformative agent goes back to the Old Testament concept of *dabar* (Word) of Yahweh, which is the motor behind Yahweh's redemptive creativity. 'God said: Let there be light and there was light.' (Gen. 1.3) This was the pattern of God's creation. God said the Word, and so it became.

St John seizes upon the Genesis concept of the creative Word and identifies it with Christ who is, according to God's new covenant, the agent of new creation (John 1.1-5). Preaching the Word is therefore not an indulgence in self-expression but an invocation and transmission of the creative and transformative grace of our Lord Jesus Christ. To evangelise is to initiate the process of new life and conversion. The evangelist is thus an icon of the creative and transformative Word, the Christ. By virtue of this iconic identity, the evangelist, who is the medium of the message, becomes the message. In true evangelism the unity between the medium and the message is realised. The evangelist thus literally incorporates the good news and becomes a facilitator of the kingdom values of love, hope, justice, healing, restoration, shalom, and integrity of creation.

We cannot divorce the ministry of evangelism from the ministry of kingdom-making any more than we can distinguish the heat of the fire from its light. Therefore it would be fallacious to have evangelism and mission as two different vocations, evangelism confined to the ministry of broadcasting the good news, and mission seen as the umbrella term to include all the good works to nurture kingdom values. This fallacy would see some as concerned only with evangelism and others engaged only in so-called kingdom-making activities. Conventional Euro-American missiology has thus relieved evangelists of the onus of engaging in the praxis of their own proclamation. This dichotomy between *kerygma* and praxis, between evangelism and mission, between being and doing, between faith and works, between Jesus of history and Christ of faith, has been instrumental in not allowing the Church to live up to its vocation of following Jesus, the historical 'man for others'.

This brings us to the missiological problem of the endemic incongruity between the preached word and the praxis in the life of the evangelist. Evangelism is the call to participate in the struggle to build Christ's kingdom, to be living stones to form the building of which the cornerstone is Christ himself. From the context of the shanty towns of Peru, Gustavo Gutierrez observes:

> If I lived complacently with three meals a day, a siesta, and a secure life, untouched by what is going on around me, then climb into the pulpit on Sunday and tell the people 'God loves you', what I say will sound hollow, like a clanging cymbal. The challenge of the gospel is its power to transform me and my attitudes and my whole way of life, so that my words will be truly meaningful to those to whom I

27

proclaim it. It is good news only if it really makes sense to them in their concrete lives.'[26]

Our other-worldly understanding of salvation in Christ has left us with a complete divide between the Church and the world. The Church is regarded as the body of Christ, the spiritual realm, as against the world, which is profane, secular and outside the scope of God's reign. So we Christians are supposed to be in the world, but not of the world. The world is a passing phase and so of the world one may say: 'Here we have no abiding city.' According to this world-negating perspective, the goal of evangelism would be to rescue souls from the choking trammels of the world and to guard the fortress Church against the earthiness of the work-a-day reality. Or a more condescending goal of evangelism would be to reform the world, to tinker with its structures in order to make it slightly more tolerable so that the Church could co-exist with it.

However, an escapist, conformist and reformist doctrine of mission could hardly be normative for the worldwide Church during the Decade of Evangelism. The only viable stance of the Church *vis-à-vis* the fallen world will be to redeem it and so that it may become a sacrament of Christ's indwelling grace. The Church's biddings will be for the kingdom to come on earth as it is in heaven. The Church should strive for nothing short of what the Eastern Orthodox Church doctrine calls *theosis*, the very divinisation of the secular and profane structures of the temporal world. The goal of all authentic evangelism for the year 2000 will be to reclaim the world as God's realm. In Bonhoeffer's luminous phrases:

> ... so to utter the word of God that the world will be changed and renewed by it. It will be a new language perhaps quite non-religious, but liberating and redeeming—as was Jesus' language; it will shock people and yet overcome them by its power; it will be the language of a new consciousness and truth, proclaiming God's peace with men, and the coming of his Kingdom.[27]

The evangelist leads the Church in renewing the world in imitation of Christ. Transformation is at the very heart of the nature of the incarnate second person of the Trinity. The divine mystery of the change in substance is the crux of Christology.

The incarnate Christ on Mount Tabor (Matt. 17.1-8, Mark 9.2-8, Luke 9.28-36), in company with Moses and Elijah representing the law and the prophecy of the old covenant, shows forth his glory as the new Messiah and becomes transfigured. The dazzling change in his appearance is momentary but is essentially an outworking of the potential for transformation inherent in Christ's nature.

In the Transfiguration we have the foretaste of the total change that transpires in the resurrection, when Christ returns from the dead and walks the earth in his risen body—healing, teaching, bestowing shalom, fishing, cooking breakfast. This represents the final phase of transformation during his earthly ministry. When the evangelist proclaims Christ crucified and resurrected, (s)he in effect proclaims and initiates transformation of the Church, people, the world and its structures.

Finally, the evangelist bears witness to the Christ of the Parousia when an entirely new order shall come into being, with a new heaven and a new earth, a new Jerusalem, where there shall be no more death, mourning, crying or pain; every tear shall be wiped away, and the old order of things shall pass (Isaiah 26.8-9, Revelation 21.1-4). Preaching the second coming of Christ, the evangelist keeps alive the hope of this continual process of the dawning of Christ's kingdom revolutionising all of God's creation.

Evangelism is, then, to journey with Christ and to proclaim him as the one who at different junctures in his earthly and transcendent ministry becomes glorified, transfigured and resurrected so that the groaning creation, which his heavenly Father so loved, may also, like him, become glorified, transfigured and resurrected.

Eucharist as Proclamation

'Whenever you eat this bread, then, and drink this cup, you are proclaiming the Lord's death until he comes' (1 Cor. 11.26).

The incarnate, transfigured, resurrected and parousial Christ, the paradigm of transformation of individuals and social structures, is also the same Christ who is present in the Eucharist as the earthly elements of bread and wine are transformed into the divine substance of his Body and his Blood. The Eucharist prefigures and proclaims the kingdom of Christ. It also tangibly provides spiritual nourishment for those engaged in the bitter struggle to build the kingdom. However, this vision of the Eucharist as a sacramental paradigm of the kingdom, where the fellowship of the faithful shares everything in a spirit of shalom, justice and grace, has too often become lost in our Christian liturgy. For many the breaking of the bread has degenerated into a trite ritual devoid of any element of urgency to invoke and invite the Holy Spirit into the broken structures of our world so that they may be healed, consecrated, and made whole. The operative words of the epiclesis are seldom taken in their full incarnational sense.

Justice is at the very heart of the Eucharist. Without the political shalom the sacrament becomes a sham. That is why the Revd Adam Cuthand, a Native American priest of the Anglican Church of Canada, condemns institutional racism condoned by established religion in sacramental terminology: 'Racism is an outward and visible sign of an inward, invisible disgrace.'[28]

It is the task of the evangelist to bear witness to the transformative and regenerative power of Christ ever present in the Eucharistic community. Evangelism is inconceivable without a networking of relationships which knit a sacramental fellowship, breaking and sharing bread not only in the holy sanctuary, but also out at the equally holy crossroads, worksites and slums. Proclaiming Christ entails participating in this challenging Eucharistic koinonia. For David Morland, the fact of transformation in the Eucharist means that

> the risen Lord is actually present, incarnate, flesh and blood in our world. The presence is dynamic, powerful, transforming. It is the act of a jealous lover who will brook no rivals . . . whose will is to shape the community celebrating it into His Body, to make it Holy; an instrument here and now of 'good news' in the world.[29]

The evangelist who is not in Eucharist solidarity with God's people would fail to witness to the Christ indwelling in the whole excruciating process of transformation preparing for the kingdom. The people proclaim no cheap triumphalism, but the hope of a better world as they celebrate the death of Christ, a death that took place outside the city gates among the meek and the marginalised. By preaching the salvation from the blood of the

Innocent One, the evangelist contends against principalities and powers. This lays the Church open to the fate of her Master. Shall we go forth and accept this challenge? Else, the Lord may well have to raise up his evangelists from bare stones (cf. Matt. 3.9) to proclaim the good news of the *ecclesia semper reformanda atque transformanda*.

Notes and References

I am greatly indebted to the Revd Jayant S. Kothare from the Diocese of London for the many invaluable suggestions he made during the writing of this paper.

1. Bishop Anthony Russell in *The Door*, the Diocese of Oxford newspaper, March 1990.
2. *Bonds of Affection, Report of Proceedings of ACC-6*, Badagry, Nigeria, 1984, p. 58.
3. Ibid.
4. *The Truth Shall Make You Free: The Lambeth Conference 1988*, p. 43.
5. *Trustworthy and True: Pastoral Letters from The Lambeth Conference 1988*, p. 20.
6. *Mission in a Broken World, Report of ACC-8*, Wales, 1990, pp. 11-12.
7. John de Gruchy, *Cry Justice*, London, Collins, 1986, p. 30.
8. *The Road to Damascus. Kairos and Conversion*. London, CIIR, 1989, p. 8.
9. Albert Nolan, *God in South Africa: The challenge of the gospel*, London, CIIR, 1984, p. 100.
10. *Evangelical Witness in South Africa* (Evangelicals Critique their own Theology and Practice), Dobsonville, 1986, p. 9.
11. See, for example, James Cochrane, *A Balance of Forces: The Church in the South African Context*, London, CIIR, 1990.
12. Albert Nolan, 'Evangelism, Mission and Evangelization', *Grapevine*, Johannesburg, CPSA, no. 30, December 1990, pp. 7-8, 9, 10.
13. Quoted in *Church Times*, 16 March 1990.
14. This was written as a rejoinder to the Roman Synod of 1974 on the theme of evangelization. *Evangelii Nuntiandi* (Evangelization in the Modern World), no. 30.
15. *Road to Damascus*, p. 7.
16. *The Kairos Document: Challenge to the Church*, Revised second edition, Johannesburg, Skotaville Publishers, 1986. For comparable material from the National Council of Churches in the Philippines see *Transformation of Church and Society*, Tugon, vol. VI, no. 2, 1986, and *Theology, Politics and Struggle*, Tugon, vol. VI, no. 3, 1986.
17. Op. cit.
18. *A Relevant Pentecostal Witness*, Chatsglen, South Africa, 1988, p. 10. Right-wing religion is defined as 'the use of Christian symbols, doctrines and rituals to legitimise and promote reactionary and oppressive political and economic objectives': Editorial, C. Villa-Vicencio, *Journal of Theology*

for Southern Africa, no.69. December 1989. This issue is devoted to right-wing religion in South Africa.

19. Nolan, *God in South Africa*, pp. 76-77.
20. *Bishopscourt Update*, 14 February 1991.
21. *Kairos Document*, pp. 9-16. See also Charles Villa-Vicencio, *Trapped in Apartheid*, Maryknoll, New York, Orbis Books, 1988, and James Cochrane, *Servants of Power: The Role of English Speaking Churches, 1903-1930*, Johannesburg, Ravan Press, 1987.
22. For a historical overview see John de Gruchy, 'From Cottesloe to Rustenburg and Beyond', *Journal of Theology for Southern Africa*, no. 74, March 1991, p. 21.
23. For key extracts from the Rustenburg Declaration see *ICT (Institute for Contextual Theology) News*, vol. 8, no. 4, December 1990.
24. *The Observer*, Canada, October 1986. For further information see Janet Hodgson and Jayant Kothare, *Vision Quest: Native Spirituality and the Church in Canada*, Toronto, Anglican Book Centre, 1990, pp. 144-152.
25. Archbishop Michael Peers, quoted in 'Evangelism must avoid past abuses', Editorial in the *Anglican Journal*, January 1991, p. 7.
26. Gutierrez cited in *'Christian Tasks in Contemporary Japan'*, translated by Ruben L.F. Habito, *Japan Christian Quarterly* Spring 1990, pp. 93-97.
27. Dietrich Bonhoeffer, *Letters and Papers from Prison*. (enlarged edition) New York, Macmillan, London, SCM, 1971, p. 300.
28. Quoted in *Saskatchewan Anglican*, May 1990.
29. David Morland, 'Oxford, Thaxted and World Poverty', in *Essays Catholic and Radical*, edited by Kenneth Leech and Rowan Williams, London, Bowerdean Press, 1983, p. 233.

3

COMPASSIONATE SERVICE
TO THE NEEDY

Sharing in the Compassion of Christ

James Ottley

On a dangerous sea coast where shipwrecks often occur there was a crude little lifesaving station. The building was just a hut, and there was only one boat but the few devoted members kept a constant watch over the sea, and with no thought for themselves went out day and night tirelessly searching for the lost. So many lives were saved by this wonderful little station that it became famous. Some of those who were saved, and various others in the surrounding area, wanted to become associated with the station and give their time, money and effort for the support of its work. New boats were bought and new crews trained. The little lifesaving station grew.

Some of the members of the lifesaving station were not happy that the building was so crude and poorly equipped. They felt that a more comfortable place should be provided as the first refuge for those saved from the sea. So they replaced the emergency cots with beds and put better furniture in the enlarged building. Now the lifesaving station became a popular gathering place for its members, and they decorated it beautifully and furnished it exquisitely, because they used it as sort of club. Fewer members were now interested in going to sea on lifesaving missions, so they hired lifeboat crews to do this work. The lifesaving motif still prevailed in this club's decoration, and there was a liturgical lifeboat in the room where the club initiations were held. About this time a large ship was wrecked off the coast, and the hired crews brought in boatloads of cold, wet, and half-drowned people. They were dirty and sick, and some of them had black skin and some had yellow skin. The beautiful new club was in chaos. So the property committee immediately had a shower house built outside the club where the victims of ship-wrecks could clean up before coming inside.

At the next meeting there was a split in the club membership. Most of the members wanted to stop the club's lifesaving activities, because they were an unpleasant hindrance to the normal social life of the club. Some members insisted upon lifesaving as their primary purpose and pointed out that they were still called a lifesaving station. But they were finally voted down and told that if they wanted to save the lives of all the various kinds of people who were shipwrecked in those waters, they could begin their own lifesaving station down the coast. They did.

As the years went by, the new station experienced the same changes that occurred in the old. It evolved into a club, and yet another lifesaving station was founded. History continued to repeat itself, and if you visit the sea coast today, you will find a number of exclusive clubs along that shore. Shipwrecks are frequent in those waters, but most of the people drown.[1]

The parable depicts the dangers that continuously confront the Church. In our understanding and interpretation of the mission and ministry of the Church, regardless of the country or culture, the Gospel message must always be clear as it addresses the needs and fears of the people whom we are called to serve. The Church should never become a comfortable club for those who are afraid of taking risks. We have but one option, to respond with compassion to those in need, those whose lives are affected by people who have power and the ability to make decisions which control production and distribution, to prolong or extinguish life, or to make life more difficult.

I live in Latin America. Therefore much of what I say is influenced by my experience here and my understanding and interpretation of the Gospel in this place at this time. In Latin America we are faced with a world that is turned upside down—a world where, if the trends continue, there will be death for many. The hardship of the international debt and the proposed long-term solutions translate into greater poverty, suffering and death for many people in the short term. The debt and the ever-present problems of health (cholera is again facing us), malnutrition, housing, education and human rights are seemingly insurmountable. We must somehow find the way out.

In the movie, *The Poseidon Adventure*, there is a scene where one of the actors attempts to find a way out of a ship that has capsized. An old priest comes to him and, as they are climbing an artificial Christmas tree to get through the galley, and maybe to safety, asks him the question, 'What is up there?' The man responds, 'I am not sure, but down there is death. Certain death. Up there is an opportunity for life, and, if we go together, the possibility is greater, since we may be able to help each other and, if we stick together, we may very well find the way out, to life.' We must find the way out together. Together, we can support each other in our search for love. Togetherness is not a bilateral conversation, but the act of standing together.

The mission of the Church is our response to God's call to reach out to the situations in which we find ourselves. For Mark, mission signifies the inauguration of the Kingdom. 'The time is fulfilled, and the Kingdom of God has come near; repent, and believe in the good news' (Mark 1.14-15). This inauguration brings with it a battle against evil. Healing and exorcism are seen as signs of the power of God against the kingdom of Satan. In Matthew, the mission of the Church is related to teaching, preaching and healing. Jesus commissioned his disciples to proclaim the good news, saying, 'Go therefore and make disciples of all nations, baptizing them in the name of the Father and the Son and of the Holy Spirit, and teaching them to obey everything that I have commanded you' (Matt. 28.19-20). And the second part of that great commandment is: 'You shall love your neighbour as yourself' (Matt. 22.39). For John, mission is a direct response to God's call: 'As the Father has sent me, so I send you' (John 20.21). Luke, however, ties mission and ministry together in a unique way. In Luke 4.18-19 we read:

> The Spirit of the Lord is upon me, because he has anointed me to bring good news to the poor. He has sent me to proclaim release to the captives, and recovery of sight to the blind, to let the oppressed go free, to proclaim the year of the Lord's favour.

It is fair, it seems to me, to say at this point that the mission of the Church has to do with proclamation of the good news of Christ, and his sacrificial reconciling offering on behalf of the world. It has to do with baptism, with the setting apart and sealing of the people of God. It calls on us to teach, share our stories and share the story of Christ. It is our response to the poor, to those in need, to the sick, to those in prison, to the voiceless and powerless. Its primary focus is justice and peace in the world.

The Anglican Consultative Council explains it this way:

The mission of the Church is therefore:
1. To proclaim the good news of the kingdom;
2. To teach, baptise, and nurture the new believers;
3. To respond to human needs by loving service;
4. To seek to transform unjust structures of society (*ACC-6*, 1984, p.49)

In recent years, I have watched how Panama and many other Central American countries are torn asunder by one critical situation after another: the war in El Salvador; the unending conflict in Guatemala and Nicaragua; the sanctions and then the invasion of Panama; the international debt, resulting from loans with flexible interest rates, which have since risen about four times above the original amount. The pressure levelled on the so-called Third World to reschedule the loan has placed even more hardships on our countries. Thus, we find ourselves in a very precarious position, as we minister to refugees, as we attempt to respond to human rights violations, and analyse policies put in motion by national and international governments.

How do we then, in the face of injustice and military oppression, of the struggle for human rights, and of exile and persecution, sing the 'Lord's song?' It is difficult, but not, however, impossible because of our awareness of our preciousness in the Lord's sight. It is his compassion that gives us strength and enables us to minister to our sisters and brothers with compassion in this world.

I tell you, my friend, do not fear those who kill the body, and after that can do nothing more. But I will warn you who to fear: fear him who, after he has killed, has authority to cast into hell. Yes, I tell you, fear him! Are not five sparrows sold for two pennies? Yet not one of them is forgotten in God's sight. But even the hairs of your head are all counted (Luke 12.4-7).

We are indeed precious in God's sight. All human beings are precious in God's sight. Presbyter Gustavo Gutierrez puts it this way: 'Our basic problem today is not Bonhoeffer's, how to speak of God to the "adult" of the twentieth century, but how to tell the poor, the voiceless, the exploited, that God loves them.'

The preciousness of life of the people of God is the purpose, the reason why we have been called to *service*, and is the basic element of our mission and ministry in the world today. This means that all our actions, especially those that affect the lives of others, must not simply be judged as to whether or not they are logical and rational, but whether or not they respond to the needs of the majority of the people. The issue it seems should be an ethical and moral one, not one of power.

> The common good is principally the good of the majority. It is the product of an option for the great violated, oppressed masses; in theory and practice, democracy must begin with the marginalized. When you start with the poor, you realize how urgent it is to prioritize human rights: the right to life and the means thereto—physical integrity, health, housing, employment, social security, education must come first. Other rights, less urgent than these, will indeed be human rights, but they will be defined from a point of departure in these even more basic rights. And here we have the concrete evidence that human rights actually coincide with a limitation of privileges of the powerful. In order to safeguard the rights of the weakest, in order that all together may be able to create and enjoy a life of justice and communion, some limitations must be placed on the rights of the mighty.[2]

Our call as Christians is to care for one another, is to build community, is to care for the deprived, to proclaim in word and in deed the Good News of God in Christ. Christ must be proclaimed as Lord and Saviour. We must somehow be willing to 'let go' and 'let Christ be.' We must be willing to let go of our personal pride, and ambitions, let go even of our illusions of ourselves.

There is one mission and that mission is Christ's mission. By nature of our baptism, we have been given the privilege to participate in that mission, reminded often 'that in as much as you have done it to one of these who are members of my family, you did it to me.' (Matt. 25.40, NRSV). We are all one in Christ, called into community, to share each other's burden, to wash one another's feet, to live a life of compassion and service. Someone has well said, that it is not on bicycles that we will be saved. Not on bicycles, with 'walkmans' belting away music in our ears—in our own privileged world all to ourselves—but rather in *buses*, holding each other's hands, being transformed and transforming in our shared experiences. We will be saved through living in relationships, justly, touching, reaching out with all our being to those around us and rejecting no one. We have to reach beyond our communities, neighbourhood and nations to be in solidarity with our sisters and brothers in a broken world, especially those in places like South Africa, the Middle East, Africa, Asia and Latin America.

We learn from the cradle that, as Christians, we are charged with the responsibility of evangelisation—sharing the good news with others, especially with the poor and oppressed. But what is so 'good' about the good news, especially for the marginalised and victimised people who inhabit our planet in vast numbers which multiply daily? The news isn't all that good unless it comes through both word and deed and brings relief to the suffering.

Our never-ending challenge in interpreting the Bible and attempting to ensure that God's will, not man's will, be done, is to apply the message and the teaching to our current reality and context. The aforementioned scriptures leave no doubt as to the challenge and responsibilities of Christians to evangelise. The statement of the Anglican Consultative Council is straight-forward and challenging. The ongoing debate is, how, when, where and with whom do we evangelize in today's world?

Is it *enough* to tell the poor that there is hope in Jesus Christ and an after-life for those who believe in him; that, if one believes, s/he will be liberated from pain and suffering and reap heavenly rewards? I think not. Is it *enough* to have discussion groups in our churches and raise our own awareness of the conditions of our brothers and sisters who live and die in poverty? I think not. Is it *enough* actively to evangelize in our own communities and neighbourhoods, personally contacting people and explaining to them the hope of a new way of life? I think not. While all of these are important aspects of evangelisation, standing alone, they do not meet the needs of the reality and context of life in the world today, especially in Latin America.

The Decade of Evangelism calls us to focus for a defined period of time on spreading the good news. Its primary focus is not, or should not be, one of bringing more people into the fold—increasing the numbers of people sitting in the pews. That will happen if we are doing it right. It is the challenge and the opportunity for the Church to serve and to address, headlong, the injustices that are taking lives at an early age and destroying our societies. No Christian today has the luxury of sitting in the 'club house' and wringing her/his hands in despair over the global situation. This crisis demands immediate action. There is no doubt that the Gospel message demands that we stand together with the poor. So evangelisation is both telling the good news and making sure that the good news is realized for all of us, especially the voiceless and powerless people in our societies, North, South, East and West. We are all responsible for fighting the fight. There are many who believe that the Church in the South has a clearer understanding of the Gospel message and of the fullest meaning of evangelisation. Our understanding is born out of the reality of our collective experiences. But we in the Southern hemisphere cannot fight this fight alone. We did not get into our situation by ourselves and we cannot get out of it by ourselves.

Part of the good news for us as Christians is that we can stand together with God and each other and we do not have to stand alone. Part of the good news is that the Church can make a difference if we are willing to join forces globally and speak out against structural injustices and their devastating impact on people, especially people in the Third World. The good news demands that we seek justice in all aspects of our lives and societies. The good news places a burden on all of us, especially the articulate, to think, speak, and act with social and political awareness, most importantly in the areas of human rights, economic justice and the insidious policies of low intensity conflict.

The good news is that some people continue to choose the option of sitting in the air-conditioned comfort of the 'club house.' They read the morning newspaper account of the spread of cholera, guerrilla attacks in the suburbs, projected starvation in a drought-stricken country and the most recent suggestion about how to restructure the international debt. At best, they shake their heads, feeling powerless to make an impact, and move on to the sports page. They either don't know how to respond or don't accept the fullness of the Gospel challenge to bring the good news to the poor.

Here, in Latin America, we do not have the luxury of turning to another page in the newspaper and going on to something else. The reality of our situation does not leave the front page for a moment and we are forced to speak and act, or perish. While some may view evangelisation as a basic requirement of our faith, and a way to increase the size of the Church, we, here, see it as essential to the survival of the people of God. We have to make an option for the poor—or who else will? We have to speak about injustice and human rights abuses—or who will know they happened? We have to put human reality into the formulas for the long-term debt reduction—or who will know that the poor will suffer even more? We have to question Northern economic and conflict policies which directly affect our well-being—or who will understand the linkages and begin to chip away at their sources in the North? I want to be clear that, North, South, East and West, the Church has been addressing and will continue to address the situation in the Third World. But I am calling for a more concerted and intentional effort of evangelisation that works not only to carry the good news to the poor and address the manifestations of poverty, but also targets the real causes of poverty—structural injustices, social and economic.

It seems imperative to me that every member of the Church should become aware of the intricate web of economic, defence and trade policies in their countries and how they impact the lives of people half a world away. Let us educate ourselves on the role and the impact our country has in the global crisis. Read, discuss and strategise about what you and your congregation can do about social and economic injustice. There are many excellent sources of information, some of which I have listed at the end of this chapter. 'The rich get richer and the poor get poorer' is a true statement, not just a saying. War and poverty are political issues and of concern to every Christian.

Every Church member should become an active evangelist by raising the awareness of public policy-makers about structural injustice. In doing so Church members are choosing to stand together with the poor and fight the fight.

The story is told of the young elephant who met some lost travellers in the desert. 'O travellers,' he said to them in a tender voice, 'where do you come from, and where are you going? Have you lost your way in the desert? Tell me, O men, that I may help you in some way.'

So happy were the men to hear these friendly words that they fell on their knees before him. 'Beautiful one,' they said, 'we have been driven from our country by our King, and have roamed through the desert for many days. Not a drop of water have we found to drink, nor food to give us strength. Help us, O dear one,' they cried; 'help us.' 'How many are you?' asked the elephant. 'We were one thousand,' they replied, 'but many have perished on the way.'

The elephant gazed at them. One was crying for water, another asking for food. 'You are weak, O men,' he said, 'and the next city is too far for you to reach without food and drink. Therefore walk towards the hill which stands before you. At its foot you will find the body of a large elephant which will provide you with food, and nearby runs a stream of sweet water.'

When he had thus spoken he ran over the burning sand and disappeared as he had come. 'Where did the great elephant go?' they asked themselves. 'And why did he run at such a pace?' Straight to the hill he went, to the same hill he had pointed out to the men; but he took another way, that the men might not see him going. He climbed to the top of the hill and then from its highest point, in a mighty jump, his beautiful body crashed to the ground below.

When the men reached the spot they gazed at the giant-like form and a great fear seized them. 'Is this not our dear elephant?' exclaimed one among them.

'This face is the same face, the eyes, though closed, are the same eyes,' said another. And they all sat in the sand and wept bitterly.

After some time one among them spoke. 'Companions,' he said, 'we cannot eat this elephant who has given his life for us.' 'Nay, friend,' said another, 'If we do not eat this elephant, his sacrifice will have been useless, and we shall die before reaching another city. Thus we shall not be helped, nor shall the wish of our elephant be fulfilled.'

The men spoke no more but bent their heads in the burning sand and ate the meat with tears in their eyes. And it made them strong, very strong, so that they were able to cross the desert and reach a town where their troubles came to an end. They never forgot the great elephant, and they lived happy ever after.[3]

We need to reach out to the lost, to the alone, to the frightened. We need to offer hope, hope that is based on the reconciling act of God, who in the fullness of time sent forth his Son, to preach, to teach, to suffer, to die, to be the bearer of forgiveness and redemption. This is the story which has become our story. The story of life over death—of Easter. The story of love, of *compassion*.

The people of El Salvador, despite civil war in which many have lost their daughters, sons, husbands and wives, and have suffered all the degradation and frustration of a war, can still say *Primero Dios* 'God first.' At a recent meeting I attended, I asked a group of Salvadorians, 'How can you, in the face of what you have been through, still say *Primero Dios*, God first? Some of you have lost your children, your husband, your sister, your mother— food is scarce, life is miserable, how can you say *Primero Dios?*'

One woman said: 'When I say *Primero Dios*, it means I have faith in God.' Another said: 'It means that I know that, despite those who support and wage war, I know that God loves me.' Another said: 'I know that God is the creator of all things. He is just, he is compassionate and in the end he will triumph over all evil.' They know that God responds fully with his grace and compassion to those in need, especially in moments of great tribulations and trials.

I began with a parable and I will close with another, which I believe sums up the major thoughts I have been trying to present in this paper:

1. that the poor should be made to know that God loves them;

2. that Holy Scripture provides us with a clear understanding of our mission and ministry to the world—a mission which is based on service and compassion to the needy;

3. that in order to carry forward a mission, it is imperative that sacrifice be understood as part of it. We must deprive ourselves of all things that inhibit our full participation in our life with Christ—selfishness, personal ambitions, competitiveness, power and greed;

4. that we are called to live in community and it is that community wherein we share our gifts and talents, especially with those in need;

42

5. that it is by the grace of God that we are who we are. Life that is nurtured in Holy Eucharist, sent forward into the world for service; sharing in community, reflecting on his story and our story, as we prepare ourselves to move out into the world in service and love.

A large number of people are huddled together under a large, food-laden table. They can smell the food, but all they see is the underside, the base of the table. All they receive are the few crumbs that fall beneath the table. Only a privileged few are seated around the table enjoying the fullness of nature's bounty. Some are totally unconscious of what is happening underneath the table. Others are dimly aware of it and occasionally pass down some crumbs to those below. But several of those at the banquet know well enough who is under the table. They are doing their best—and worst—to keep things as they are. They don't want anyone to spoil their meal. They don't want to upset the status quo. A person enters the room. He walks across to the table. But instead of taking his place in the seat of honour, he stoops down and gets under the table. He sits with the hopeless people down below and shows them his love and concern. With him as their head, they begin to have hope. God loves them! He has something good in store for them. They join in small groups to sing, pray and study his word. In time they will be ready to come out from under the table, to join the privileged few in common meal around the table.

Notes

1. This parable originally appeared in an article by Theodore Wedel, 'Evangelism—the Mission of the Church to those Outside Her Life', *The Ecumenical Review*, October 1953, p.24. The above is a paraphrase, as appeared in *Basic Types of Pastoral Counselling*, by Howard J. Clinebell, Jr. Abingdon Press, 1966.
2. Leonardo Boff, *When Theology Listens to the Poor*, p. 55.
3. Noor Inayat Khan, *Twenty Jataka Tales*, pp. 105-107.

Bibliography

Barry, Tom and Deb Pruesch. *The Central American Fact Book.* Grove Press Publications. Broadway, New York, 1986.
Boff, Leonardo. *When Theology Listen to the Poor.*

Dorr, Donald. *Spirituality and Justice.* Published in Ireland by Gill and Macmillan Ltd, 1984. Goldenbridge, Dublin 8. Published in the USA and Canada by Orbis Books. Maryknoll, New York, 10054

Khan, Noor Inayat. *Twenty Jataka Tales.* East West Publications Fonds, Hague, 1975.

Puls, Joan, Osf. *A Spirituality of Compassion.* Twenty Third Publication, Mystic, Connecticut.

4

INTEGRITY OF CREATION

Striving to Safeguard the Integrity of Creation and
Sustain and Renew the Ecological Life of
the Earth

Kenyon Wright

In this Decade of Evangelism, the ship of human society seems
to be sailing straight for the rocks of destruction. We have to
decide whether the central task of mission is to fill the lifeboats,
or save the ship. All we do in evangelism in this Decade will
depend on whether we see mission—and therefore evangelism as
part of mission—as centrally and primarily concerned with the
growth of the Church, or with the growth of the Kingdom, God's
rule and will 'done on earth as it is in heaven'.

The sign of the ecumenical movement has always been a ship,
surmounted by the cross and sailing through troubled and stormy
waters. Both 'ecumenical' and 'ecological' come from the same
root, the Greek word *oikos* meaning 'household'. The ship in the
symbol is not the Church alone: it is the human household, the
whole of human society on its journey through the awesome seas
of history.

Our evangelism is stunted, unbiblical and sub-Christian if it is
reduced to the tempting offer of a safe and comfortable seat in the
warm lifeboat whose name is Jesus—though in times like now,
when the storm is especially fierce and menacing, that offer of
individual escape can have great power. We are not keepers of the
lifeboats. We are called to be pilots of the vessel. We are that part
of the crew who hold the compass, who know at least something
of the true destination of the voyage, and the purpose of the real
owner.

Our evangelism is therefore a direct invitation and challenge to
others to join the company of those who know where the ship of
human society is going. It is an invitation to joy and to suffering;
to peace and to a sword; to rest and to struggle. It is not an easy

call to 'come to church' but a costly challenge to 'be the Church' in a world where that will be increasingly demanding and even dangerous.

The fundamental question is what we think the Church's Mission is: what we think the Church is for. Some years ago, I prepared for a Lent series on radio, by going out with a roving microphone to the busy shopping precinct in Coventry on a Saturday morning. A friend and I stopped passers by at random, and asked them the question 'What do you think the Church is for?' The result was occasionally hilarious—like the youth who replied in a thick Midlands accent, 'The Church—it's good for the old folks. Keeps them off the streets' More often however, replies were depressing. Almost universally, the word 'go' was used. The unchurched, the majority, simply said either 'I don't go' or in many cases 'I ought to go' Those who did belong gave various reasons for 'going to Church'. Always, the Church was seen as a building, run by professionals and providing a service appreciated by some, but unwanted by most. Not one reply presented the Church as a dynamic community, engaged in Christ's Mission of reconciling love in a world in crisis.

Anglicans have always shared a comprehensive understanding of mission as including evangelism or direct proclamation, but also having other equally important concerns. For some years, the Anglican Consultative Council and the Lambeth Conference have developed this four-part definition:

The Mission of the Church is:
1. To proclaim the good news of the kingdom;
2. To teach, baptise, and nurture the new believers;
3. To respond to human needs by loving service;
4. To seek to transform unjust structures of society.[1]

In 1990 the Anglican Consultative Council, meeting in Wales, agreed to add a fifth affirmation, namely:

5. To strive to safeguard the integrity of creation and sustain and renew the life of the earth.[2]

The title Decade of Evangelism is perfectly legitimate and acceptable provided we do not confine our understanding of evangelism to the first part of the above definition, but recognise that it must relate to and even include all the other parts. It might, however, have been less open to misunderstanding, and perhaps to a partial response, if we had from the start called it a Decade of Transformation. Not only does this word more clearly include all the elements of our mission, but it is an idea often used by the ACC meetings in the past. The 1988 Lambeth Conference issued a pastoral letter entitled 'On the Gospel and Transformation' in which they said:

> Some lay stress on inner personal change, others on social and political change. But increasingly, as we have learned from each other and grown in commitment to each other, we have recognised the real task into which Jesus Christ is sending us all. We must hold these varied emphases together in one gospel and one witness in the one Body.

They base this view of the transformation as the goal of mission on an earlier statement which defined it as

> a change from a level of human existence that is less than that envisaged by our Creator, to one in which we are fully human and free to move to a state of wholeness, in harmony with God, with fellow human beings, and with every aspect of our environment.[3]

When the Ecology Clause (as some called the fifth affirmation above) was added in 1990, with its recognition that the integrity of creation is part of mission, this was not a trendy addition, tacked on in an attempt to be fashionable or to jump on the green bandwagon. It was not the expression of some passing contemporary concern, somehow peripheral to the central truth of the Gospel of Jesus Christ. It was rather the belated recognition that, for our time at least, our 'cry for creation' might well be the very central test of our obedience, of the reality of our faith, and the validity of our mission.

Our growing awareness of the enormous threat of environmental disaster and ecological crisis, and our discovery of the fact that 'everything connects', that all the great life-or-death issues of our day are closely intertwined, are compelling us to see afresh an ancient truth embedded deep in our faith and in the Bible; a truth that is the litmus test of the authenticity of all our missionary effort, and of the Decade of Evangelism.

That truth is simply that God's Mission in Christ is concerned with the renewal of creation, and the reconciliation and unity of all things in the universe. What does this mean, for our reading of the gospel and of the time of crisis in which we live, and for our mission today?

Suggested answers to that question are set out in the six propositions that now follow, under three broad headings.

One warning is important. Like all theses, these are not meant either to be swallowed whole, or to be instantly rejected; they are to be tested, verified, or changed.

Wherever you live—and this book may well be read in all the continents—you are asked to apply strict tests to the propositions that now follow. Do they ring true to the Gospel and to the Bible? Are they realistic about the world of struggle and hope in which you live? Are the ideas for the Church's mission possible, or adaptable, in your real situation? Quite simply, do they work?

Above all, can you add to these, or change them, to make your own 'Confession for Crisis'?

I invite you to respond, so that this Chapter can one day be rewritten, not out of the thoughts of one person, but out of the deep collective experience and wisdom of our great world community. That is an exciting prospect.

Mission and Creation—The Concept in the Bible and the Gospel

(The Integrity of Creation—Defining Health)

PROPOSITION 1:

That the integrity, or unity, of all creation is God's gift and purpose, and a central part of the mission of Christ.

> He has made known to us his hidden purpose—such was his will and pleasure determined beforehand in Christ—to be put into effect when the time was ripe: namely, that the universe, all in heaven and on earth, might be brought into a unity in Christ. *Eph.* 1.10

The world created by the Word of the living God, brought to birth in harmony out of chaos by his Spirit, is not just the scenery for the drama of salvation and mission, not just the backdrop for our human story, which will one day be rolled up and thrown away.

It is given to us to make us human. We find our true happiness and the meaning of our lives only in proper relationships both with the *oikumene* (the world of human society) and with the *cosmos* (the world of nature). It is indeed the 'place where in the end, we find our happiness, or not at all' (William Wordsworth). The world is to be reconciled and renewed, not destroyed.

In the creation stories of Genesis, our peace, our *shalom*, is the positive well-being and health of living in harmony with God, with one another, and with nature. Justice is 'righteousness', the right relationships, evidenced by the unashamed open nakedness and vulnerability of Adam and Eve before God and each other, and their harmony with the garden.

We are happy, we are fully human, we are our true selves as God made us to be, only when we can live open to God, and in mutual dependency on the neighbours he gives us, and the earth which is our home.

The Bible ends with that harmony restored. The promise of Revelation is of *shalom* regained, but immeasurably enriched by the glory and suffering of the human story and its redemption in Christ. The heavenly city which is God's ultimate gift is a place into which 'all the nations bring their glory', where all that is good and true in the long history of human life is redeemed. It is also a place where nature itself is renewed. Through the city flows the crystal river, shaded on either bank by the tree of life, 'and the leaves of the tree are for the healing of nations'. The One who sits on the throne of history, and who is 'the same yesterday, today, and for ever' is the One who constantly says 'Behold, I make all things new'

The mission of Christ can only be understood in this context, of creation and re-creation. Christ's incarnation, death and resurrection are the turning point of human history and the beginning of the new creation. The central theme of his teaching and mission is the Kingdom (or Rule) of God. His parables are usually stories of the Kingdom, about human relationships restored. His miracles are 'signs of the Kingdom', often about the lost harmony of nature restored.

PROPOSITION 2:

That the restoration of the harmony of creation is central to the mission of the Church, and therefore to the Decade of Evangelism.

God was in Christ reconciling the world to himself ... and has entrusted us with the message of reconciliation.' *2 Cor.* 5.19

The search for unity is an important part of the mission of the Church. A divided Church proclaiming a gospel of reconciliation is a bit like a bald man selling hair restorer. It is rather unconvincing. Our divisions damage our evangelism, however, for a deeper reason. If God's will and purpose is the reconciliation and harmony of all things in the universe, if the Rule of God means the restoration of our true relationships with our fellow human beings, and with the world of nature, then the Church is called not only to be the witness and proclaimer of that wonderful news, but also to be the sign and the first fruits. People should be able to look at the Church and see there, in miniature and in hope, a model or a picture of the loving harmony with one another and with the world, which is God's will for all the earth. That is why Jesus commanded his disciples to 'Love one another, as I have loved you'. It is the clearest and most unambiguous of all his commands, yet it is the one the Church most frequently disobeys. We so often decide with whom we will have fellowship and who are our fellow pilgrims. We are guilty of saying to other members in the body of Christ, 'I have no need of you'.

Worse still, we confirm our sectarian and sub-Christian disunity, when we reduce mission to the spreading of religion and Church growth, and reduce evangelism to 'winning souls'.

The Decade of Evangelism will fail if it ignores the historical predicament of the 1990s, and if it does not help the Church towards a 'confessing' faith and a mission which presents the whole gospel for the whole person in the whole of society throughout the whole world.

The Gospel is a call to costly commitment, not an easy invitation to religious certainty.

The Church is the army of the living God, locked in mortal combat with the 'powers and principalities, the spiritual forces of wickedness in high places', not a comfortable club, a coterie of the self-satisfied saved keeping themselves spiritually warm.

The mission of the Church is a bold and dangerous witness to the Rule of God, in a world where the Prince of Darkness seems to rule, not an exercise in numbers and Church growth offering the illusion of an easy escape.

The faith is a celebration of life in all its fullness; not a religious ghetto apart from real life.

Mission and Creation—The Context in the Kairos Decade

(The Decade of Disintegration—Diagnosing the Disease)

PROPOSITION 3:

That we stand at a Kairos, a unique turning point of history, because we live on one interdependent world, which seems to be in terminal decline.

> The world is in crisis. The problems of poverty, and debt: of militarisation and mass destruction: of ecological disaster and decay: are all signs of a society and eco-system nearing collapse. 'The real danger lies in the interaction of these threats. Unless far-reaching changes are made now, the crisis will intensify, and may turn into a real catastrophe for our children and grandchildren!'[4]

Kairos is a Greek New Testament word which means time, in the special sense of 'the time of crucial choice: the moment of decision'. Our Decade is such a *kairos*.

Ours is the first generation that can literally see the world whole. Those pictures of the earth taken from the moon show us a blue crystal ball hanging in space. It is fragile, delicate, and breathtakingly, heart-stoppingly beautiful. Yet we know that the very technologies that allow us to see that incredible sight also make us the first generation that could shatter that fragile beauty for ever.

1992 is the 500th anniversary of the so-called 'discovery of the Americas' by Christopher Columbus. Some call it a celebration, others a lament. Either way, what we remember is the period of history which has created, slowly but inexorably, the first truly global civilisation. All that followed from 1492, in colonisation, the Industrial Revolution, the new technologies, and so on, has brought all of us, wherever we live, into a single global history. The world is one; we are interdependent as never before in the long human story. We live, at the end of the twentieth century, in the *kairos*, the time when our common history, and the exploitation and greed on which it is based, are reaching their

51

point of no return—when we must either find new ways of living together, or perish. One World, yes—but it is deeply divided and dangerous. The gap between the rich North and the poor South gets wider every year. It is a world of haves and have-nots, of victors and victims.

We can no longer pretend that we do not live by the gift of one another and nature. We are reminded day after day how fragile is the thread that binds our lives to that of others and of all living things. The acid rain produced in factories far away, pollutes the lakes and streams, and withers the trees in central Europe. The greedy devouring of the tropical rain forest of Brazil affects our climate. A small explosion in a nuclear plant adulterates the food and irradiates the land in countries a continent away. The seals of the North Sea die, poisoned or fatally weakened by the filth poured into it by industrial nations greedy for production. Life on earth has taken billions of years to develop, and its myriad forms and species beat the air, teem the seas and cover the land. In the next few decades it is reliably estimated that some quarter of all living species may become extinct.

But that is not the end of the story. Nature, which we have so terribly tortured and disfigured, can at last take its revenge on us—and will do so now. All life is bound together by delicate threads. We are destroying ourselves. Life is deeply threatened as never before in the entire long story of the human race. That is the simple fact of our situation. It is the context of our mission today.

In the time it takes to read this chapter alone, some 1500 children have died of hunger or related disease, while the nations of the world have together spent about $US2 million on weapons of death.

This day, and every day till things change, at least one species of animal, bird or insect becomes extinct. This week, and every week till things change, about $2000 million is added to the enormous burden of debt that crushes the poorest nations, and ensures that the net flow of wealth is actually from the poor to the rich.

This month, and every month till things change, tens of thousands of people are imprisoned, cruelly tortured or killed by oppressive governments or their agents.

This year, and every year until things change, tropical rain forests the size of Belgium are destroyed and lost for ever, with catastrophic effects on climate.

This decade, and every decade till things change, the level of the sea will rise significantly as a result of global warming, with potential disastrous consequences for large areas of the planet, such as Bangladesh.

Our generation is caught in a trap, victims of our own violation of justice and peace and of the integrity of nature itself.

Bertold Brecht wrote: 'Those who laugh have not yet heard the terrible news'.

If we as Christians can still echo the laughter and the joy of creation, it is not because we are blind to the grim suffering and the terrifying prospects of our time. It is because, through it all, we hear the voice of the living God setting before us, with appalling clarity, darkness and light, chaos and harmony, death and life, and calling us to choose life.

PROPOSITION 4:

That our Kairos, our time of choice and decision, is God's offer of new life and renewed relationships to his world—and that he calls his Church to share his love and pain.

The Church is the place where human existence is clarified and understood. *Dietrich Bonhoeffer*

We are the children of Hiroshima and of Auschwitz. Both changed the world for ever. Einstein said, 'We have unleashed the power of the atom, and nothing will ever be the same again'. Hiroshima symbolises the knowledge and power we possess, to destroy the earth. Even after much-heralded cuts in strategic weapons, there are still enough weapons stored to destroy all life on earth not once, but twenty times over. But the ecological crisis is even more subtle. To destroy the world through the collapse of the delicately balanced environmental systems, we simply have to do nothing. It is enough for us just to go on as we are.

Auschwitz symbolises our terrible ability to demand our own comfort or prosperity or well-being, at the expense of the misery, the exploitation, and even the lives, of others.

Taken together, our power and our greed bring death.

53

Paradoxically, our very power makes us powerless; our greed makes us vulnerable. We are the first generation to know that we can never again be safe *from* one another; we can only be safe *with* one another; to know that if we go on exploiting the earth as we are, then it may take a terrible vengeance on our children. God is saying to our age that we can never again be safe or happy, except by new relationships of trust and caring, both individually and corporately.

That is God's word to our world—and we must speak it. It will not be popular, for it threatens many of the vested interests of power and money, of politics and economics, but it must be said, for it is the word of life for our time. It is God's chart for the strange new land into which he has brought us—a land of terrifying fears and towering hopes, which our forebears could never have imagined.

It is also God's word to his Church. Our mission is to sing the Lord's song.

But how shall we sing the Lord's song in this strange land? That question has always two answers. The first lies in the true nature of the land. Even the strangest of lands is the Lord's. Our estranged and melancholy society is to be reclaimed, and we are to be the signs of its intended harmony. Its discordances and wild music will never prevent us from singing the Lord's song—and through the very worst of its cacophony that song will always be heard and never drowned out. Under the jarring discords and screeching disharmonies of our time, the land has never forgotten the song of creation which called it into being, and waits to hear again the music of the spheres. Our lips may sing that song with faltering voices and uncertain tones, but it is still the Lord's song—and the land will recognise it and rejoice.

The second reason lies in the true quality of the song. The Lord's song is not composed for calm places. Its music was made for the maelstrom of life in all its strangeness. It can never be an easy song to sing—for its very harmony is a threat to the competing discords. It is a music of judgement and shame as well as of an unearthly beauty. It is a song that may ravish with gladness but may ravage with shame. It is a song that may give its hearers peace or a sword. It is a song to comfort the disturbed and to disturb the comfortable. It is a song to call forth ecstatic joy or incandescent anger. It can never be a comfortable song to sing. The Lord's song is not a soothing lullaby but a heart-rending lament. It is not a comfortable hymn of complacent assurance sung in a closed church. It is a song of defiant hope of soaring faith and of costly love, sung in the market place in the slums and on the highways of life.

The Lord's song rings out when Archbishop Romero in Latin America, or Archbishop Janani Luwum in Africa, give their lives because they refuse to be blind to the corruption and evil in their societies. It rings out when thousands of unknown men and women are tortured, imprisoned and killed because they will not bow the knee to the false gods of money and power.

Though the God of truth may demand of us different sacrifices, of one thing we may be sure. To sing the Lord's song in this world, is to invite trouble.

Mission and Creation—the Content of Evangelism today

(Decade of Transformation—A Mission of Healing)

PROPOSITION 5:

That the Decade of Evangelism demands a 'Confessing' Church: we witness by what we say and what we are.

True 'Confession' involves both penitence and bold witness. In Nazi Germany, the Confessing Church which stood bravely and at such cost against the racism and idolatry of the State (and frequently also against their fellow Christians who wanted a quiet life, and to 'keep the Church out of politics') recognised clearly their own complicity and responsibility for what had happened, before they took their stand on the gospel against an inhuman society.

We live both as beneficiaries and victims of a global system which is death-dealing. The structures within which all of us live are economically unjust, politically unparticipative, and ecologically unsustainable. Our mission of reconciliation demands that we both speak up and live differently. But we can only do so when we recognise the corporate sin of which we are part; when we repent.

1992, the 500th anniversary of the start of the modern era, is a good time to begin the search for a 'common history' and reconciliation of memories, which will enable us to see the part we have played, either as victims or oppressors, or both, in building and sustaining this unjust and dying world. The Anglican Communion can foster this, by bringing together those from the North, who have largely benefited by the world system, with those from the South, who have largely been impoverished and marginalised by it. Only together can we reach a common view of the history that has brought us to this decade of Crisis. Only together can each of us repent in any real sense. Only together can we develop a 'Confessing Word' for our time.

In 1934, when the dark clouds were already gathering over Europe, the young Dietrich Bonhoeffer, who was to die a martyr ten years later on Hitler's orders, called on the Churches to recognise the signs of the times, and to speak 'a word that cannot be overlooked'. In 1959, in the worst time of the Cold War, Hromadka of Czechoslovakia founded the Christian Peace Conference and called on it 'to speak an even more decisive word'.

In the 1990s there has never been greater need for that word that cannot be overlooked, for that even more decisive word. How can we speak it? How can we 'think globally but act locally'?

Bonhoeffer sealed his fate when he proclaimed in the Nazi state 'Those who do not cry for the Jews, dare not sing Christian hymns'. It was more than a declaration of war on the evil of his society; it was a witness that no true Christian could avoid that war, that it was the very test of the reality of faith.

What is the equivalent for us? What is the test of our mission and faith? I suggest 'Those who do not cry for creation dare not sing Christian hymns'.

To cry for creation is to cry for the poor. Globally, it means clear witness against the debt crisis, and a call for a 'year of Jubilee' in which at least the poorest nations are absolved. It means creating a new international economic order. Locally, it means standing with the poor, the powerless and the marginal in our own neighbourhood, whoever they are.

To cry for creation is to cry for the planet. Globally, that means using the Earth Summit (the UN Conference on the Environment and Development, 1992) as a focus for developing a Christian Charter for Creation, in which we speak together against vested interests that prevent the nations from acting radically enough to save the future. Locally, it means developing personal 'pledges for the planet' about our own lifestyle and behaviour, and also working as congregations and other groups to build 'projects for the planet'.

The Anglican Consultative Council, meeting in Wales, in 1990 (ACC-8) summarised and commended the Covenants worked out at the World Convocation on Justice, Peace and Integrity of Creation in Seoul in 1990, as a basis for our mission, as follows:

SUMMARY OF THE SEOUL COVENANTS

1. For a just economic order at local, national, regional and international levels for all people; for liberation from the bondage of foreign debt that affects the lives of hundreds of millions of people. The Churches should support economic systems and policies that ensure that the dignity of people and creation comes before profit, and make themselves free of complicity with unjust economic structures.

2. For the security of all nations and peoples, for the demilitarisation of international relations, for a culture of non-violence as a force for change and liberation. The Churches should witness to the love of God through, among other things, practising our Lord's call to love the enemy, through giving up any theological or other justification of the use of military power, through developing justice and peace ministries.

3. For preserving the gift of the earth's atmosphere to nurture and sustain the world's life; for building a culture that can live in harmony with creation's integrity; for combating the causes of destructive changes to the atmosphere which threaten to disrupt the earth's climate and create widespread suffering. The Churches can develop new theological perspectives concerning creation and the place of humanity within it, and join the global, local and personal efforts to safeguard the integrity of creation.

4. For the eradication of racism and discrimination at national and international levels for all peoples. The Churches should take the lead in breaking down walls which divide people because of their ethnic origin, by implementation of such principles in the policies and practices of Churches and Church-related bodies.

These affirmations and covenants should be seen as the beginning of a process opening out to the Christian Churches, congregations and movements, and even further to all people struggling for justice, peace and the integrity of creation. This Act of Covenanting in Seoul constitutes an open invitation to enter into a network of mutual commitment for action.

PROPOSITION 6

That the Decade of Evangelism demands a strategy of mission which is both local and global: we witness by what we do.

> Our fight is not against human foes, but against cosmic powers, against the authorities and potentates of this dark world, against the superhuman forces of evil in the heavens. Therefore, take up God's armour . . . *Eph.* 6.12, 13

We are at war. We need a battle plan. A cry for creation is not enough, we need a plan for the planet. Any local congregation which takes seriously all five of the elements of mission defined by ACC (quoted at the start of this chapter) will seek, if at all possible with other Churches in the area, to build up a mission strategy which has clear goals, and which explicitly includes all five dimensions.

Some of the questions that will have to be asked to build such a battle plan, are:

(a) Have we clear objectives in each of the five areas? (Broadly they are: proclamation; nurture; service; social transformation; environmental integrity). Can we set, say for the next year and for the next five years, well-defined goals in each of these areas?

(b) What resources have we, especially in people? Who in our community have special interest in, or expertise in, any of these five areas? Where are our people in the secular community? (This is best done together with all the Churches of an area, since the presence and influence of the laity in the secular structures is seldom possible on a purely denominational basis.) With what non-church bodies should we be allied?

(c) Can we build up, together with our neighbour churches of all denominations, a team ministry, with division of labour, i.e. with at least one minister or appointed worker taking responsibility, within a commonly agreed strategy, for one of the five areas of mission? (This could be further developed and refined as the strategy works. The task of the appointed 'minister' would be to pioneer in the area allocated, and to 'equip the saints', i.e. to work with groups of lay people to develop their ministry and give it both a firm biblical base and social relevance.)

(d) Can we build up, again with others if possible, a Mission Council which will constantly review progress towards the goals we have set in each of the five areas; which will regularly carry out Mission Audits to see how we are getting on?

(e) Can we identify the larger church agencies, at national and international level, to which we have to relate, so that our local strategy can be related to the larger picture, so that we can really 'act locally but think globally'?

(f) How can we influence the Churches in our region or nation as a whole, to develop the same kind of holistic strategy of mission, so that our plan will be part of an effective network?

ACC-8 in 1990 sent a letter to children all over the world, signed by the Archbishop of Canterbury. It quoted a former Archbishop, Michael Ramsey, who said that when we meet God, one of the most important questions he will ask is, 'Did you enjoy the world I made for you?'

I think there will be another question too. God will ask, 'Did you take care of it? Did you protect and renew the world of which I made you the temporary stewards? If you did, I give it to you to enjoy for ever.'

DOXOLOGY

Having committed ourselves in Covenant Solidarity and
Mindful that we are stewards of Creation
We join with all you made
To celebrate your glory
And to sing your praise

Glory to God
Who in the Beginning created all things
And saw that it was good

Glory to Jesus
Firstborn of the new Creation
And Redeemer of all

Glory to the Spirit
Who in the beginning hovered over the water
And who fills Creation with your love.

RAINBOW'S END

When the dove cannot fly for its oil-clotted pinions;
When the olive branch withers in soil made impure;
When the rainbow corrodes in a rain become acid;
Will the promise still hold, will the earth yet endure?

If nuclear winter assassinates springtime,
If seedtime made barren brings harvest no more;
If day turns to darkness and dusk without dawning;
How long, Lord, how long will the earth yet endure?

When the safety of some means the misery of many;
When the affluent feast on the flesh of the poor;
When debts must be paid through the weeping of children;
Will his mercy remain, will the earth yet endure?

Where the lamp of the Lamb lights our guilt and our gladness;
Where the book of God's judgement at last is unsealed;
Where the clear crystal river of mercy is flowing;
There the tree of life blossoms, the nations are healed.

Notes

1. *Bonds of Affection*, Report of Proceedings of ACC-6, 1984, p. 49.
2. *Mission in a Broken World*, Report of Proceedings of ACC-8, 1990, p. 101
3. Report of International Evangelical Consultation on the Nature and Mission of the Church, Wheaton, Illinois, 1983, quoted in *Bonds of Affection*, p. 58.
4. Justice, Peace and Integrity of Creation document, Seoul.
5. *Mission in a Broken World*, Report of Proceedings of ACC-8, 1990, p. 103.

Section II
Mission in Context: Church and World

5

ECUMENICAL CONTEXT

Alexander Malik

Missio Ecclesiae is Missio Dei

The mission of the Church, (*missio ecclesiae*) is none other than the mission of the triune God (*missio Dei*). And God's mission was and has always been directed towards the world—the world which he created himself through his Word, the Logos: 'In the beginning was the Word . . . all things were made through him, and without him was not anything made that was made' (John 1.1-3). God sent the Son to save the world: 'God so loved the world that he gave his only begotten Son, that whoever believes in him should not perish but have eternal life' (John 3.16). And again, 'God was in Christ reconciling the world unto himself' (2 Cor. 5.19). God as Creator, Redeemer and Sanctifier is a God of mission and his mission is directed towards the world. He has been choosing individuals or groups or nations to do his mission but the mission has always been inclusive of the whole world— all the nations of the whole world. God is the Creator and Father of all people; he cares and provides for them, extending his blessing to all (cf. Gen. 12.3). The Noahic Covenant is made with all the living creatures of the world (cf. Gen. 9.1-17). Though God chose Israel for his purposes, nevertheless the blessings were for all the nations of the world. In the course of history, Israel comes to realise that her election has a universal meaning (cf. Isa. 2.2-5; 25.6-8, 60.1-6, Jer.3.17, 16.19). The Church's mission as God's mission has to be directed towards the whole world and not only to one part or region or continent. The Father sent the Son and the Son sent the Church: 'As the Father has sent me. I am sending you' (John 21.21). Again Jesus said, 'As you sent me into the world, so I have sent them into the world' (John 17.18). This sending is into the whole world, to all the nations of the world. Jesus Christ told his disciples to preach the Gospel to all the nations of the world: 'Go into all the world and preach the Gospel to the whole Creation' (Mark 16.15). 'All authority in heaven and on earth has been given to me. Go therefore and make disciples of all nations' (Matt. 28.18, 19). Jesus Christ promised the early Church, 'But you shall receive power when the Holy Spirit has come upon you; and you shall be my witnesses in Jerusalem and in all Judaea and Samaria and to the end of the earth; (Acts 1.8).

As the mission of the Church is basically the mission of God, it has to be universal. The early Church realised this quite early and opened the doors of the Gospel to the Gentiles as well, though not without pain. The coming of the Holy Spirit on the Feast of Pentecost and the preaching of St Peter on that day is in itself demonstrative of the fact that the Gospel has to be preached to all nations (a number of them were present on that day) and to the whole world (Acts 2).

Ecumenism and Mission are Intrinsically Related

The world as it has always been consists of different peoples, nations, regions, religions, cultures, languages, etc. And the mission of the Church has to do with all of them. Its context is basically ecumenical—*oikoumene*, the whole inhabited earth. Over the years, ecumenism has come to be regarded as unity movements in different Christian Churches and denominations. The World Council of Churches has played a significant role in these unity movements. Now because of the ecumenical movement there are a number of united Churches in the world. Moreover a greater understanding of goodwill, co-operation, conciliation and dialogue has grown between different Churches and confessional families. This is all due to the realisation that the divided Church is a disgrace to the holy name of our Lord and a great hindrance in the Church's mission and evangelism. The Lord's high priestly prayer clearly links the unity of the Church with its mission and evangelism (John 17.20, 23). But ecumenism has a wider dimension as well, the unity of humanity. Jesus Christ as the Word of God (Logos), the Incarnate Word, stands central to this unity of humanity. St Paul talks about it a number of times, especially in Eph. 1.3-14, and Col.

1.15-23. In Christ 'the whole fullness of deity dwells bodily' (Col. 2.9) and 'from his fullness have we all received' (John 1.16). The 'only Son, who is in the bosom of the Father' (John 1.18) is 'the beloved Son, in whom we have redemption ... For in him all the fullness of God was pleased to dwell, and through him to reconcile to himself all things, whether on earth or in heaven, making peace by the blood of his cross' (Col. 1.13,14,19,20). It is precisely this uniqueness of Christ which gives him an absolute and universal significance, whereby, while belonging to history, he remains history's centre and goal: 'I am the Alpha and the Omega, the first and the last, the beginning and the end' (Rev. 22.13). Even otherwise, Jesus Christ as Logos is principal agent of God's creation and the invisible image of God (Col. 1.15), in whom all humanity has been created. Thus, whether it is ecumenism within the Church or outside the Church, Jesus Christ stands central and he is central in the mission of the Church as well. Therefore ecumenism and mission are intrinsically related.

The ecumenical context in which the Church's mission has to be carried out should challenge and inspire her, yet there are questions and reservations being raised which weaken the Church's missionary thrust, especially towards non-Christians. Some people wonder: is missionary work among non-Christians still relevant: has it not been replaced by inter-religious dialogue? is not human development an adequate goal of the Church's mission? does not respect for conscience and for freedom exclude all efforts at conversion? is it not possible to attain salvation in any other religion? are not different religions alternative routes to God? why then should there be missionary activity? These are genuine and valid questions and need an exploration and response from the Church. In this chapter we shall pick up the most basic question, i.e. are different religions alternative routes to God?, as it has a deep bearing on the whole question of the Church's mission in an ecumenical context. As I have practically lived all my life in an Islamic country and environment, I will restate that question as, is Islam an alternative route to God? Our exploration of this question should be applicable to other religions and religious contexts as well.

Is Islam an Alternative Route to God?

This is one of the most important questions to be asked especially in the context of the Church's mission and evangelism. If it is an alternative route, then why bother to engage in mission and evangelism and sharing of the Gospel? The Muslims would find their way to God, even through their own route. Let us then leave them alone and not disturb them.

Therefore there are many who advocate cessation of all activities connected with mission and evangelism as far as the Islamic world is concerned. And there are still others, who may not propagate the same message in that direct way, yet they may very well question the Church's frenzied pleadings for the fulfilment of the Great Commission. Thus, they call such people with contemptuous labels like evangelicals; fundamentalists; conservatives; intolerant; bigoted. But if Islam is not a route to the Christian God, then what are we doing for mission and evangelism in the Islamic world? Why has mission in the Islamic world not met with success as in some other cases? Why does it still bother and baffle the mind of the evangelism experts, that mission in the Islamic world is not only difficult but next to impossible? All of these questions arise in our minds when we think about the question, Is Islam an alternative route to God?

The question has three very important words: alternative, route and God. It is perhaps assumed that Christianity is also a route. We leave it to the reader to ponder, meditate and judge whether Christianity is a route or not. But what about other religions? Is Hinduism an alternative route to God? or Buddhism, or Zoroastrianism or Sikhism or Taoism? You may say that you are not sure, but the case of Islam is quite different from Hinduism or Buddhism, as it stands in line with the other two commonly called monotheistic religions, Judaism and Christianity. Then, we would ask, is Judaism an alternative route to God? You may say Yes to Judaism and perhaps No to Islam, or at least you may say that you are not sure. Does the answer to the question have to be either Yes or No? I personally think not. There are questions in answer to which we should not promptly say either Yes or No. Even Jesus did this when faced with such questions. Once when he was asked, 'Who is my neighbour?' by an expert of the Law, he narrated to him a story and left it to him to find the answer (Luke 10.25-37). On another occasion, also, he did the same when asked, 'Is it right to give tribute to Caesar?' Jesus did not reply with a simple Yes or No. Again he said, 'Render therefore to Caesar the things that are Caesar's and to God the things that are God's' (Matt. 22.21) and left it to his hearers to find an answer.

We are also going to do the same. We will share with you some insights on the question and leave it to you to make your own judgement.

The question 'Is Islam an alternative route to God?' basically focuses our attention on the question whether the God of Islam and the God of the Gospel is the same. Here again the answer cannot be either Yes or No. It must be both Yes and No. God, as the subject of all *theologies*, is necessarily the same, but what the adjectival language says about him differs widely. Since it is the purpose of adjectives to define and describe the subject, the disparity in the adjectival language enters into the sense of the subject. But that the disparity concerns the one subject, i.e. God, is evident. For otherwise it would not be realized as disparity and there would certainly be no point in noting it. St Paul brings to the people at the altar in Athens the news of the God of the Gospel. But, he says, he is the God they 'ignorantly worship'. He does not ask them to deny the intention of their worship, but to find it informed into the truth of God in Christ. What he denies is the predicate 'unknown'. 'Whom you in ignorance worship him declare I unto you'. God, then, the subject of all theology, is one, both for Islam and Christianity. We may name him Allah or Baghwan or Yahweh. As to the predicates, as faith affirms and worship ascribes them, Muslims and Christians in part say Yes to each other's predicates, and in part say No. Let us see briefly similarities and differences of understanding of God as it has a bearing in finding an answer to our question, 'Is Islam an alternative route to God?'

The Christian doctrine of the nature of God is as put in the Athanasian Creed, 'We worship one God in Trinity and Trinity in Unity'. Holiness and love are basic characteristics of God. All this means that God is person, and by person it means that he relates himself firstly within the Godhead as Trinity and then with other persons. He communicates, chooses and acts in relationship with other persons.

67

In the Islamic concept of God oneness (unity) of God is central. Holiness and love are also not absent, but in meaning and content are quite different from what is generally understood by Christians. In Islam, because God is holy, he is set apart; therefore a lot of emphasis is laid on the transcendence of God. God is wholly other, nothing is like him, and since he is wholly other he cannot enter into relationship with human beings or others. And even if he enters into relationship it is one of Master and servant or Judge and the judged and not of Father and son. This in itself presupposes the doctrine of man. This relationship which Christians talk about is possible as 'man is created in the image of God'. St John says in his prologue of all those who believe in Christ that he will give them the power to become the children of God (John 1.12). For men and women to become children of God is unthinkable and even blasphemous in the Islamic understanding of God; whereas in Christian understanding God is depicted as father and even husband. A relationship concept is basic to the Christian understanding of God.

Christians are usually criticised for having a very low and base doctrine of man because of the doctrine of original sin. In Islam man is not inherently evil. He can know God and strive to achieve paradise by obeying the commandments of God and following the straight path as told by the Prophet (P.B.U.H.) and exemplified by his Sunnah (life). This leads us into the doctrine of sin and salvation, as all of these are linked with some aspect of the doctrine of God.

In Islam sin is essentially a violation of the law, of God-given instructions concerning religious duties and moral and social obligations. In Christianity, on the other hand, sin is often described in relationship terms; grieving the Holy Spirit; spurning the Son; being at enmity with the Heavenly Father. In Romans, for example, Paul speaks of men being in sin and under the dominion of sin. Fundamentally sin is a state of separation from God, rather than a series of violations of his regulations. It is to say that before sin is an act, it is a state—state of separation, broken relationship. In Islam the order is reversed. It is not that we become God's people, and therefore act in a particular way, but that we act in a particular way and are therefore God's People. The practices, the obedience to regulations are of primary importance. It is by keeping these that the believer pleases God and draws near to him, and that he receives the best in this life and in the next. Sin for the Christian, then, is anything that offends God and therefore breaks relationship with him, while sin for the Muslim is a wandering from God's laws that results in judgement.

Similarly, both Christianity and Islam have a doctrine of salvation, and yet the understanding of it in their respective religions is very different. Muhammad Abdul Quasem, in his book *Salvation of the Soul and Islamic Doctrine*, describes the difference and recognizes that, in the Christian faith, 'salvation is primarily deliverance from sin'. 'Such deliverance', he says of Christianity, 'is possible here and now and when it is made actual a new spiritual life is achieved through which the interrupted communion of fellowship with God is restored'. Such is not the case in Islam.

Islamic teaching is that sin stands between man and God, no doubt, but he is not dead in it; so no new birth of the Spirit is needed; he must, however, repent. Man is not by nature in a position from which he needs to be redeemed. He commits sin of which he must repent; his repentance is not salvation, but only a means to it. Salvation is safety from punishment from sin in the life after death.[2]

Quasem is clear here on the differences between the Christian and Islamic ideas of salvation. The Christian seeks salvation from the state of sin itself and the Muslim from punishment for sin. This, of course, reflects the ideas of sin discussed briefly above. The Christian wants to be saved from the state of sin because that state is one of being cut off from relationship with God. The Muslim does not see the need for such a salvation since he does not believe that he has fallen out of relationship. Indeed, he does not believe this relationship to be possible. He sees man as he is—fallen, out of relationship with God—and assumes that to be his natural state.

He may, therefore, seek to approach closer to God, and to know more of him, but he will not seek the restoration of a relationship which he does not believe ever existed. Salvation, for him, if we can rightly use the word in this context, can imply only an escape from judgement (punishment) and an entry into paradise, And since the nature of salvation in the two religions is different, the means of attaining it is also different. This should suffice to make my point.

The point is that to the question 'Is Islam an alternative route to God?' we will have to ask, route to which God? If you are asking about the God revealed in Jesus Christ, then it is certainly not. But Islam is a route to its own God. It has an alternate God and an alternate system based on that God. You will say but God is one: how could there be a Christian god or Hindu or Islamic god? Yes, of course, God is one. But when our perceptions of this one God differ, we end up believing in different 'gods'. Then our world views or views about life also become different. And this difference is then reflected in liturgy and worship, morality and ethics, theology or anthropology, etc. Simply to say that since the reality of God is one, all religions are the same or different routes to the same God, is based on an incorrect theological perspective and is characterised by a religious relativism which leads to the belief that one religion is as good as another. We do not subscribe to this view. (This is a very old view, that it is like looking at one sun with different coloured glasses, and so, if you are looking with green glasses, the sun seems to you green, and so on). This is an over-simplification of a very complex problem.

Woe to us if we do not preach the Gospel

If Islam, or any other religion, is not a route to the God revealed in Jesus Christ—the Christian understanding of God, what bearing has that on our mission and evangelism? We have no other choice except to share the Good News of Jesus Christ with the Muslims and others. This may be difficult but not impossible. Pluralism of religions in our present day ecumenical context is not a new phenomenon. It has existed since olden times. It was there in the Old Testament period, in the time of the prophets, and of Jesus, the early Church, and has been there throughout history in one form or the other.

But all along the Church has not compromised with other religions or routes or systems. It really cannot if it is faithful to the Gospel of Christ. Yes, we know that people criticise us for being exclusive and even call us fanatics but the Lord whom we follow has been making exclusive claims for himself. He said, 'I and the Father (God) are one. No one can come to the Father except by me.' 'He, who has seen me, has seen the Father (God).' And then, not only he, himself, but also his disciples have been making exclusive claims for him.

If we go back to the beginnings of the Church, we find a clear affirmation that Christ is the one Saviour of all, the only one able to reveal God and lead to God. In reply to the Jewish religious authorities who questioned the apostles about the healing of the lame man, Peter said, 'By the name of Jesus Christ of Nazareth, whom you crucified, whom God raised from the dead, by him this man is standing before you well . . . And there is salvation in no one else, for there is no other name under heaven given among men by which we must be saved' (Acts 4.10,12). This statement, which was made to the Sanhedrin, has a universal value, since for all people—Jews and Gentiles alike—salvation can only come from Jesus Christ.

The universality of this salvation in Christ is asserted throughout the New Testament. St Paul acknowledges the risen Christ as the Lord. He writes: 'Although there may be so-called gods in heaven or on earth—as indeed there are many "gods" and many "lords"—yet for us there is one God, the Father, from whom are all things and for whom we exist, and one Lord, Jesus Christ, through whom are all things and through whom we exist' (1 Cor. 8.5,6). One God and one Lord are asserted by way of contrast to the multitude of 'gods' and 'lords' commonly accepted. Paul reacts against the polytheism of the religious environment of his time and emphasizes what is characteristic of the Christian faith: belief in one God and in one Lord sent by God.

In the Gospel of St John, this salvific universality of Christ embraces all the aspects of his mission of grace, truth and revelation: the Word is 'the true light that enlightens every man' (John 1.9). And again, 'no one has ever seen God; the only Son, who is in the bosom of the Father, he has made him known' (John 1.18; cf. Matt.11.27). God's revelation becomes definitive and complete through his only-begotten Son: 'In many and various ways God spoke of old to our fathers by the prophets; but in these last days he has spoken to us by a Son, whom he appointed the heir of all things, through whom he also created the world' (Heb. 1.1,2, cf. John.14.6). In this definitive Word of his revelation, God has made himself known in the fullest possible way. He has revealed to humankind who he is. This definitive self-revelation of God is the fundamental reason why the Church is missionary by her very nature. She cannot do other than proclaim the Gospel, that is, the fullness of the truth which God has enabled us to know about himself.

Christ is the one mediator between God and humankind: 'For there is one God, and there is one mediator between God and men, the man Christ Jesus, who gave himself as a ransom for all, the testimony to which was borne at the proper time. For this I was appointed a preacher and apostle (I am telling the truth, I am not lying), a teacher of the Gentiles in faith and truth' (1 Tim. 2.5-7, cf. Heb. 4.14-16). No one, therefore, can enter into communion with God except through Christ by the working of the Holy Spirit.

Christ's one, universal mediation, far from being an obstacle on the journey towards God, is the way established by God himself, a fact of which Christ is fully aware. Although forms of mediation of different kinds and degrees are not excluded, they acquire meaning and value only from Christ's own mediation, and they cannot be understood as parallel or complementary to his.

Having such a clear testimony and message, we should not be ashamed of the Gospel of Christ. While respecting the beliefs and sensitivities of all, we must first clearly affirm our faith in Christ, the one Saviour of humankind, a faith we have received as a gift from on high, not as a result of any merit of our own. We say with St Paul, 'I am not ashamed of the Gospel: it is the power of God for salvation to every one who has faith' (Rom. 1.16). Christian martyrs of all times—including our own—have given and continue to give their lives in order to bear witness to this faith, in the conviction that every human being needs Jesus Christ, who has conquered sin and death and reconciled humankind to God. The Church cannot fail to proclaim the Good News of Jesus Christ.

To the question, 'Why mission?' we reply with the Church's faith and experience that true liberation consists in opening one's self to the love of Christ. In him, and only in him, are we set free from all alienation and doubt, from slavery to the power of sin and death. Christ is truly 'our peace' (Eph. 2.14), 'the love of Christ impels us' (2 Cor. 5.14), giving meaning and joy to our life.

Mission is an issue of faith, an accurate indicator of our faith in Christ and his love for us.

The temptation today is to reduce Christianity to merely human wisdom, a pseudo-science of wellbeing. In our heavily secularized world a gradual secularization of salvation has taken place, so that people strive for the good of man; but man who is truncated, reduced to his merely horizontal dimension, needs the vertical dimension as well. We know, however, that Jesus came to bring integral salvation, one which embraces the whole person and all humankind, and opens up the wondrous prospect of divine filiation. Why mission? Because to us, as to St Paul, 'this grace was given, to preach to the Gentiles the unsearchable riches of Christ' (Eph. 3.8). Newness of life in him is the Good News for men and women of every age: all are called to it and destined for it. Indeed, all people are searching for it, albeit at times in a confused way, and have a right to know the value of this gift and to approach it freely. The Church, and every individual Christian within her, may not keep hidden or monopolise this newness and richness which has been received from God's bounty in order to be communicated to all humankind.

I know that at times we are blamed for restricting and limiting the working of the Holy Spirit. People say, how can we limit or chain the Holy Spirit only to the Church or to the Christian Gospel.? The Spirit of God is free to work where he likes or wills. We do not deny this truth. But the conclusion drawn out of this we reject.

The Holy Spirit of God is also called the Spirit of Christ, and his main function is to witness to Christ. 'When the Spirit of Truth comes, he will guide you into all the truth, he will glorify me ...' (John 16.12-14). 'He will bear witness to me.' The work of the Holy Spirit is not to witness to someone else but only to Jesus Christ. He works in the Church and outside, even where Christians have failed to witness for Christ.

Therefore the universal free working of the Holy Spirit should not deter us from bearing witness to Jesus Christ for which we have been called and commissioned. 'God so loved the world that he gave his only begotten Son ...' (John 3.16). 'Go into the world and baptise all nations ...' (Matt. 28.19). 'When the Holy Spirit has come upon you ... you shall be my witnesses not only in Jerusalem ... and to the end of the earth' (Acts 1.8). God's loving the world and the disciples going into the world include all, people of faith or no faith.

Different Ways of Engaging in Mission

Mission is a single but complex reality, and it develops in a variety of ways. Among these ways, some have particular importance in the present situation of the Church and the world. Some of these briefly are as follows:

(a) PROCLAMATION (*KERYGMA*)

The Church is especially called to proclaim the Good News of Jesus Christ—that in Jesus Christ God has inaugurated a new humanity through which people can become sons and daughters of God: 'He came to his own home, and his own people received him not. But to all who received him, who believed in his name, he gave power to become children of God; who were born, not of blood nor of the will of the flesh nor of the will of man, but of God' (John 1.11-13). The salvation is offered to humanity not on the basis of merit or good works but by grace in believing and accepting Jesus Christ as personal Lord, God and Saviour. This Good News of Jesus Christ can be proclaimed to the world through preaching or writing or in other ways.

(b) SERVICE (*DIAKONIA*)

Like her Master and Lord, the Church has to engage herself in serving others: 'The Son of Man has come not to be served but to serve' (Matt. 20.28). Service (*diakonia*) is a practical form of proclamation. Actions usually speak louder than words. Even in the life of Jesus, we see that practically every miracle of his aroused a response from his audience. The Church's different ministries of education, health care, adult literacy, emergency help, drug prevention, etc. are different forms of *diakonia* and are significant ways of mission. ACC-6, while discussing 'Mission and Ministry' rightly says:

> Just as Jesus was able to hold together proclamation and service, the Church must also hold the two together in the right balance. It is no longer necessary to put a wedge between evangelism and social responsibility, and Christians should not be divided between those

who see mission primarily as evangelism and those who identify mission with activities designed to relieve human suffering. Evangelism and social responsibility are partners. It is this vision of man as a social being as well as a psychosomatic being which obliges us to add a political dimension to our social concern (John Stott, *Christian Mission in the modern world*, p.29). Jesus did not only heal the sick, he also challenged scribes and Pharisees on issues of Sabbath laws and fasting (Matt. 2.23-28), dietary laws and divorce (Mark 10.2-12). The healing of a man who was sick for 38 years and his commanding him to break the Sabbath, was a challenge to the selfish structures of the society which put more emphasis on observing (unnecessary) Sabbath laws rather than seeing a man who had suffered for 38 years healed. We are, therefore, called upon not only to do acts of mercy but to go to the root causes of human suffering and struggle for justice with hope of transforming the unjust structures which are by and large responsible for human suffering. Christ's followers are called, in one way or another, not to conform to the values of this world but to be a transformed and transforming people. (Romans 12.1-2, Eph. 5.8-14).'[3]

(c) FELLOWSHIP (*KOINONIA*)

The Church is a fellowship (Koinonia) of believers and it is sanctified by the presence of Christ: 'where two or three are gathered in my name, there am I in the midst of them' (Matt. 18.20). Moreover, 'the powers of death shall not prevail against it' (Matt. 16.18b). She is the Body and Bride of Christ. Christ himself is the head of this fellowship (*koinonia*) and its life stream. Any person who falls out of this fellowship (koinonia) dries and eventually dies (John 15). Corporately and individually her members are the temple of the Holy Spirit (1 Cor. 3.16-17, 2 Cor. 6.16) and as such she is a sign and symbol of God's presence in the world. She is a chosen means of imparting health, healing and wholeness. Her activities of liturgy and worship, prayer and petition, teaching and preaching, confession and counsel, baptism and confirmation, solemnisation of marriage and family life, and more particularly celebration of the Holy Eucharist, and funeral and burial services are but just a few means of proclamation of the death and resurrection of Jesus Christ. Again, all these activities, which may seem to some just a routine, could become excellent ways of proclaiming the Good

News of Jesus Christ. Church planting thus becomes an important missionary activity.

(d) WITNESS (*MARTURIA*)

Christians are especially called to be witnesses of Christ, from whom they take their name. People put more trust in witnesses than in teachers, in experience than in teaching, and in life and action than in theories. As the Greeks came to see Jesus (John 12.21), so also in the present-day world people want to see Jesus in the lives of individual Christians, families and ecclesial communities and congregations. We are called to live a simple life, imitating Christ and taking him as a model. God's love expressed in the life and person of Jesus Christ has to be exhibited and demonstrated in the day to day lives of Christians individually and corporately. The evangelical witness which is most appealing is that of concern for people, and of charity towards the poor, the weak and those who suffer. The complete generosity underlying this attitude and these actions stands in marked contrast to human selfishness. It raises precise questions which lead to God and to the Gospel. A commitment to peace, justice, human rights and human promotion is also a witness to the Gospel when it is a sign of concern for persons and is directed towards integral human development. St Paul exhorts the Christians to 'present your bodies as a living sacrifice, holy and acceptable to God' (Rom. 12-1), and they are called to be faithful unto death with a promise to inherit crown of life (Rev 2.10b).

(e) DIALOGUE

In an ecumenical context inter-religious dialogue is one of the significant ways of engaging in mission. As the Church's mission is basically addressed to those who do not know Christ and his Gospel and God in Christ calls all peoples to himself, inter-religious dialogue becomes a means to proclaim and present Christ. In the light of the economy of salvation, the Church sees no conflict between proclaiming Christ and engaging in inter-religious dialogue. Pope John Paul II in his Encyclical Letter says that dialogue should not in any way detract from the fact, 'that salvation comes from Christ and that dialogue does not dispense with evangelization'. He goes on further to say

> Although the Church gladly acknowledges whatever is true and holy in the religious traditions of Buddhism, Hinduism and Islam as a reflection of that truth which enlightens all men, this does not lessen her duty and resolve to proclaim without fail Jesus Christ who is the way, and the truth and the life . . . The fact that the followers of other religions can receive God's grace and be saved by Christ apart from the ordinary means which he has established does not thereby cancel the call to faith and baptism which God wills for all people.

In the same Encyclical Letter he writes:

> Dialogue should be conducted and implemented with the conviction that the Church is the ordinary means of salvation and that she alone possesses the fullness of the means of salvation . . . Through dialogue, the Church seeks to uncover the 'Seeds of the Word,' a 'ray of that truth which enlightens all men': these are found in individuals and in religious traditions of mankind. Dialogue is based on hope and love, and will bear fruit in the Spirit. Other religions constitute a positive challenge for the Church: they stimulate her both to discover and acknowledge the signs of Christ's presence and of the working of the Spirit, as well as to examine more deeply her own identity and to bear witness to the fullness of Revelation which she has received for the good of all. This gives rise to the Spirit which must enliven dialogue in the context of mission. Those engaged in this dialogue must be consistent with their own religious traditions and convictions, and be open to understand those of the other party without pretence or closemindedness, but with truth, humility and frankness, knowing that dialogue can enrich each side. There must be no abandonment of principles nor false irenicism, but instead a witness given and received for mutual advancement on the road of religious inquiry and experience, and at the same time for the elimination of prejudice, intolerance and misunderstandings. Dialogue leads to inner purification with docility to the Holy Spirit, will be spiritually fruitful . . . dialogue can assume many forms and expressions: from exchanges between experts in religious traditions or official representatives of those traditions to co-operation for integral development and the safeguarding of religious values; and from a sharing of their respective spiritual experiences to the so-called

'dialogue of life', through which believers of different religions bear witness before each other in daily life to their own human and spiritual values, and help each other to live according to those values in order to build a more just and fraternal society.[4]

Conversion and Baptism: a Missiological Issue

Both conversion and baptism are logical results of the Church's mission and evangelism. The Church invites people to accept Jesus Christ as their personal Lord, God and Saviour; and to repentance, conversion and baptism. The disciples did the same in the early Church: 'Repent and be baptised every one of you in the name of Jesus Christ . . . and you shall receive the gift of the Holy Spirit' (Acts 2.37-38). And again, after healing the lame man, Peter spoke to the crowd: 'Repent therefore, and turn again that your sins may be blotted out' (Acts 3.19). Turning again to God is conversion of a person, a dynamic and lifelong process of turning away from 'life according to the flesh' to 'life according to the Spirit' (cf. Rom. 8.3-13).

Some people raise questions about conversion and condemn it by saying that it is proselytizing. They say that it is enough to help people to become more human or more faithful to their own religion, that it is enough to build communities capable of working for justice, freedom, peace and solidarity, and thus reject any efforts of conversion. There are yet others who may say that conversion is all right but why baptise people and ask them to undergo rites which are strange, unnecessary and even dangerous, as baptism can completely alienate a person from his people, culture and environment. Therefore they encourage people to remain secret believers and reject baptism. This is particularly true of Islamic countries, where change of religion (conversion) may endanger a person's life and property. Thus conversion and baptism are lively missiological issues; and the Church needs to respond to these if we are serious about Church's mission.

As we look into the scriptures, we find that conversion and baptism are closely related. The call to repent is followed by baptism: 'Repent and be baptised' (Acts. 2.37 ff). St Peter when convinced about the conversion of Cornelius immediately went ahead with baptizing him (Acts 10.34-48). So also Philip, when he was sure that the Ethiopian eunuch was convinced about the

Good News of Jesus Christ, baptised him right there. Baptism is not something extra, rather a logical corollary of conversion. 'Conversion', says Pope John Paul II

> is joined to baptism because of the intrinsic need to receive the fullness of new life in Christ. As Jesus says to Nicodemus. 'Truly, truly, I say to you, unless one is born of water and the Spirit, he cannot enter the Kingdom of God' (John 4.5). In Baptism, in fact, we are born anew to the life of God's children, united to Jesus Christ and anointed in the Holy Spirit. Baptism is not simply a seal of conversion, a kind of external sign indicating conversion and attesting to it. Rather, it is the sacrament which signifies and effects rebirth from the Spirit, establishes real and unbreakable bonds with the Blessed Trinity, and makes us members of the Body of Christ, which is the Church.[5]

Notes

1. Kegan Paul International, 1983.
2. Ibid., p. 29.
3. *Bonds of Affection*, Proceedings of ACC-6, Badagry, Nigeria, 1984, pp. 48-49.
4. *L'Osservatore Romano*, N.4., 28th January 1991, p. 13.
5. Ibid, p. 12

6

CULTURAL CONTEXT

French Chang-Him

Introduction

Ruth from the country of Moab said to Naomi from the land of Judah: 'Where you go, I will go, and where you stay, I will stay. Your people will be my people and your God my God. Where you die, I will die. And there I will be buried.'[1]

Here was a commitment which led to a mission. The sum of both meant the embracing of and engaging with cross-culturisation. The result? God's will was fulfilled. Back in Bethlehem in the land of Judah, Ruth met and married Boaz. This is how Matthew describes the succeeding genealogy, 'Boaz the father of Obed, whose mother was Ruth, Obed the father of Jesse, and Jesse the father of King David.'[2] And Jesus Christ the Messiah was to be born of the House of David, also in Bethlehem. His incarnation in turn was to mean complete immersion into humanity and human culture.

What is culture?

Culture means 'the language, history, stories, customs, lifestyle, accumulated wisdom and religion into which we are born, by which we are shaped and through which we find our identity as human beings. Through this culture, which is not static but ever-changing, God is making us.'[3]

'Culture is what holds a community together, giving a common framework of meaning. It is preserved in language, thought patterns, ways of life, attitudes, symbols and presuppositions, and is celebrated in art, music, drama, literature and the like. It constitutes the collective memory of the people and the collective heritage which will be handed down to generations still to come.[4]

'Culture implies the totality of social structure, art and artefact, language use, recreation, the intertwining of belief and life.'[5]

Mission and Evangelism through Culture

Jesus commissioned his disciples with these words, 'As the Father has sent me, so I send you.'[6] They too were to pursue the mission, assisted by the Holy Spirit, to their society. That implied adapting themselves to different cultures. Thus later, St Paul was to become a Jew to the Jews and a Greek to the Greeks. But their mission would also mean confronting the culture where it proved to be contrary to the good news or to the righteousness of the God to whom they owed obedience. In emphasizing this point, Archbishop Edward Scott in *Crossroads Are For Meeting* says:

> The mission of the Church starts with God and his action in creation. In creation, human beings, male and female, made in the image of God, have a very distinct role. They stand within the created order as 'decision makers,' 'choosers,' 'initiators.' They are given freedom by God—freedom to seek, to know, and to do the will of God and so to become co-creators with God.[7]

Thus the Church recognises that mission is not something she does. Instead, it is rather part of being the Church, one, holy, catholic, apostolic. It is about being sent, as the apostles were.

It is realised that the question of the nature of the relationship between the Gospel and culture has been with us from the start. However, the issue has been brought to light in a fresh way for several reasons. For example, we are coming to a deeper understanding of the meaning and functioning of culture, with its complex nature. We have observed with better understanding the ways in which the Gospel has interacted with different cultures. We have become acutely aware of the problems that have arisen because the receptor cultures have been ignored or denigrated by former missionaries from the sending Churches. In consequence, the need for discernment has become imperative. As we affirm and welcome cultures as an expression of the great wonder of God's creation, we have experienced that not all aspects of every culture are necessarily good. For instance, there are certain aspects within certain cultures which oppress people and deny life, such as segregation of any form, discrimination against women, and child labour.

81

Culture and the Scriptures

Christ transcends all cultural settings. Consider the visit of Jesus to the vicinity of Tyre. A Syro-Phoenician woman whose daughter was possessed by an evil spirit begged him for deliverance. In an apparently rough way he indicated that his primary concern was his mission to Israel—'The children's meat is not for the dogs.' But when in persisting faith she is willing to wait for the children's crumbs under the table, her faith is rewarded with a commendation and healing for her daughter.[8]

As Christianity confronted and became confronted itself by the world, it shed some of its Jewish-Hellenistic acquired characteristics and acquired in turn new characteristics from its receptor cultures. At times it accepted certain elements as they were, at other times it transformed them. There were occasions when it rejected elements that were considered incompatible with the Gospel. For example, the Council of Jerusalem, which was convened to discuss the question of circumcision of new Gentile converts, brought Paul and Barnabas into sharp dispute and debate with the Pharisees. This is how James, the apostle who presided over the Council, summed up the dispute:

> It is my judgement, therefore, that we should not make it difficult for the Gentiles who are turning to God. Instead we should write to them, telling them to abstain from food polluted by idols, from sexual immorality, from the meat of strangled animals and from blood.[9]

Culture and the Spread of Christianity

With the spread of the Christian message, this process continued throughout Europe and progressively into other parts. Thus, the Western Culture which early missionaries transported to mission fields in far away lands bore certain marks of cultures inherited from other lands and nations through which the Church had passed. Obviously, new problems in understanding the relationship between the Gospel and culture arose further as later missionary enterprise carried the Christian message to the Americas, Africa, Asia, the Pacific and elsewhere. Looking back, we give thanks for the zeal, perseverance and sacrifice of the early missionaries, but we also notice how, in many cases, they in fact inhibited the Gospel from taking root in the cultural soil into which it came. Where the Gospel has been expressed in the cultural forms in which the community understood itself, its message has become a transforming power within the life of that community.

In view of the foregoing, the World Council of Churches has put forward the following recommendations:

In the search for a theological understanding of culture we are working towards a new ecumenical agenda in which various cultural expressions of the Christian faith may be in conversation with each other. In this encounter the theology, missionary pespectives and historical experiences of many churches, from the most diverse traditions (for example Orthodox and Roman Catholic churches) offer fresh possibilities. So too do the contributions made by women and young people in this search for a new ecumenical agenda.

With this background in mind we need to take specific steps:

a. In the search for a theological understanding of culture, we can do the following: share a rich diversity of manifestations of the Christian faith; discover the unity that binds these together: and affirm together the Christological centre and Trinitarian source of our faith in all of its varied expressions.

b. We need to be aware of the possibility of our witness to the Gospel becoming captive to any culture, recognizing the fact that all cultures are judged by the Gospel.

c. In contemporary societies there is an evolution of a new culture due in part to modernization and technology. There is a search for a culture that will preserve human values and build community. We need to reassess the role played by, in particular, secular and religious ideologies in the formation of culture, and the relationship between this process and the demands of the Gospel and our witness to it.

d. While we recognize the emergence of Christian communities within minority groups that affirm their cultural identity, we should pay special attention to the fact that many of these are in danger of being destroyed because they are seen as a threat to a dominant culture.

e. We need to look again at the whole matter of witnessing to the Gospel across cultural boundaries, realizing that listening to and learning from the receptor culture is an essential part of the proclamation of the Christian message.[10]

Recent Resolutions

In recent years, the question of culture in the ongoing mission of the Church has been given its rightful place prominently and firmly on the agenda of the most notable international meetings of the Anglican Communion. Several resolutions have been adopted and recommended for implementation. Here are some of them.

RESOLUTION 21 OF THE PRE-LAMBETH CONFERENCE
FOR AFRICA—JULY 1987

Dogmatic and Pastoral Concerns—CHRIST AND CULTURE

This Conference affirms that man is made in the image of God and therefore his culture has aspects of beauty fully acceptable to the Gospel. Because of the Fall, however, man's culture has aspects which the Gospel cannot condone. All cultures without exception have to be judged by the Gospel. The Church should reject any cultural aspects which are contrary to the Gospel, and uphold those aspects which do not contradict the Gospel. The African Church should make full use of its cultural heritage which can enrich her life in liturgy, ceremonies, celebrations, etc. To this end this Conference recommends:

a. That the Bible be translated into all important vernacular languages of Africa.
b. That each Province, as a matter of urgency, should prepare alternate worship and ceremonial liturgies, taking into account our cultural heritage.
c. That local Churches, planning to construct church buildings, should take into account the African ways and designs of construction.
d. That should there be a shortage of imported wine and wafers, the Provinces should sanction the use of locally produced bread and wine.[11]

The urgency for an alternative prayer book based on African cultural heritage, with room for a truly African, joyful worship, has been noted. The concept of 'community' in many non-Western cultures as against individualism, as a means of enriching the Christian faith, also needs to be borne in mind.

RESOLUTION 22 OF THE LAMBETH CONFERENCE 1988

Christ and Culture

This Conference:

a. Recognises that culture is the context in which people find their identity.
b. Affirms that God's love extends to people of every culture and that the Gospel judges every culture according to the Gospel's own criteria of truth, challenging some aspects of culture while endorsing and transforming others for the benefit of the Church and society.
c. Urges the Church everywhere to work at expressing the unchanging Gospel of Christ in words, actions, names, customs, liturgies, which communicate relevantly in each contemporary society.[12]

RESOLUTION 47 OF THE LAMBETH CONFERENCE 1988

Liturgical Freedom

This Conference resolves that each Province should be free, subject to essential universal Anglican norms of worship, and to a valuing of traditional liturgical materials, to seek that expression of worship which is appropriate to its Christian people in their cultural context.

LITURGICAL INCULTURATION AND THE ANGLICAN COMMUNION

(Findings of the Third International Anglican Liturgical Consultation, York, England, 21-24 August 1989; *Mission in a Broken World*, Report of ACC-8, 1990, pp. 172ff.)

After quoting Resolution 47 of the Lambeth Conference 1988, the Statement continues:

We have discovered the need to illustrate these principles by examples. Those given here are necessarily few, for the sake of brevity, and are also inevitably arbitrary. Consider these questions:

a. *Language*: is Tudor English anywhere appropriate today? Have countries developed local vernacular styles for liturgy? Are metaphors appropriate to the locality? Does the language exclude or demean any people on ethnic or gender or intellectual or other grounds? Are the kinds of book and the demands of reading them such that worshippers relate easily to them?—What about the illiterates?

b. *Music*: are English hymn-tunes universally appropriate? Do local musical styles provide a better cultural medium? Are local settings encouraged? Are the words of hymns, even if in translation, drawn from another culture? Is the organ all-pervasive, or are other instruments in use?

c. *Architecture*: has Gothic with nave and chancel been over-valued worldwide? Can existing buildings be imaginatively adapted?

d. *Ceremonial*: are choir-boys to wear surplices even on the Equator (and sit in those Gothic chancels)? Should robes be imported, or can they be locally designed with local materials? Are there ways in which people's existing practices can be incorporated? We heard of African dances in procession, of North American native peoples smoking the pipe of peace at the Peace, of workers in Sri Lanka bringing their union concerns and symbols into special eucharists, and the instances could be multiplied.

e. *Sacramental elements*: here there are special problems, needing more work. Should wafer bread be as dominant as it seems to be—even to the point of being imported? Should local staple food and drink supervene? How far can variations be allowed?

f. *Rites of passage*: we note the long-standing Christian Jando ceremony (male circumcision at the onset of puberty) in the diocese of Masasi, Tanzania, and its combination with confirmation and first communion. Is this a model to be copied or adapted elsewhere? Or are there other ways in which Christian initiation can be inculturated in different places? Equally, we sought examples of where local marriage customs have affected liturgy—but found few. Can such customs be more fully assimilated into marriage liturgies? The variety of culturally distinct styles of funerary customs is in process of re-discovery round the world, whether it be a Caribbean-style funeral in multi-ethnic parts of England or the Maori blessing of a house after a funeral in New Zealand.

g. *Political and Social Context*: at times Christians suffer or are oppressed, or are caught up in wars, or need to identify with the oppressed. This kind of stance, because it is their context, becomes their culture, and, if truly infusing their worship, in turn reinforces their public stance.

h. *Agapes*: Christians have gathered for meals from the start. The growing revival of agapes in our Communion we welcome, not only for the breaking down of walls between the 'sacred' and the 'secular', not simply for their fellowship aspect, but also because both these factors enable people wherever they are to be themselves with their own customs, and to be free to bring those ways into the heart of church life.

We would not want to suggest that some purely tokenist inclusion of a single local practice into an otherwise alien liturgy will suffice. Nor is it necessary for a whole liturgical event or series of events to be culturally monochrome: good liturgy grows and changes organically and always has rich marks of its stages of historical conditioning upon it, and in addition has often to serve truly multi-cultural congregations today.

In each Province and diocese Anglicans ought to examine their degree of attachment to ways of worship which are required neither by the gospel itself, nor by the local culture. We do not think that these criteria should be set aside by a loyalty to some supposed general 'Anglicanism', for every expression of the gospel is culturally affected, and what is viewed as general Anglicanism, if it can be identified, grew in a very specific Western culture.

Crossing Cultural Boundaries

Some years ago, I buried an old gentleman who had died at the age of 102 years. He had lived all his life on a little island of some 35 square miles. Just before he died, he expressed that he had only one regret—that he had never visited the prime tourist spot on his island, a botanist's paradise which nurtures the largest palms, with double nuts, and the home of the only black parrots in the world. Tourists travel thousands of miles to visit this garden. But our centenarian friend, who had walked past that place thousands of times on his way to the main village, always thinking, 'one day I shall go in', never did.

Mobility is one of the marks of our present world. Mass tourism brings financial fortunes to both industrialised, rich countries as well as to some of the poorest developing countries—and much else. Academic and cultural organisations organise educational and cultural tours and exchange projects. Sporting activities necessitate much travelling locally or abroad. Migrant workers cross seas and oceans. Ecumenical, inter-confessional and denominational conferences bring religious groups together globally. Government representatives criss-cross the globe incessantly for consultations. Famine, natural disasters, internal conflicts and wars create mass movements of refugees. Voluntary immigration makes the question 'Is this your original home?' more and more relevant in social conversation. How many times do we stop someone in a town we are visiting to ask for direction or some other information to be told, 'Sorry, I do not live here' or we as visitors get stopped for the same purpose!

There is a Chinese restaurant in almost every country in the world. You can buy yam in Montreal and rent a video filmed in Nevada in Nossi Be, Madagascar. At an international conference, most of the young people could be wearing jeans and T-shirts and know how to rap to the latest beat. Ninja turtles are currently vying for first place against Soungroula (Brer Rabbit), Tom and Jerry or Big Bird in the children's kingdom. It was the discovery of an empty tin of coke found in the middle of nowhere in a remote part of the African Continent by a tribe that could not identify it which became the focus of the story in the film 'The Gods must be mad'.

Everything is becoming so familiar in our shrinking one-world environment. The pace of life increases daily, for some. 'Fax is instantaneous and accurate. But it also makes everything urgent,' said one secretary in a busy office in Canada. 'Before, people used to write letters and wait for a reply. Now they send a fax and ask for an answer immediately.' Meanwhile, we are being conditioned and we take things for granted. In this Province, if you are five minutes late to start a service at the Cathedral in one of the Capitals, the congregation starts to get agitated and annoyed. In another part of the Province, I was held up for two days because of bad weather and rough roads, and the congregation, some of whom had walked some 50 km to the village, waited patiently for one's arrival, which was greeted with such genuine joy with singing and dancing.

Transpose the above example to other areas of international, cross-cultural boundaries. For instance, the non-verbal participation of usually articulate delegates from certain countries at meetings or conferences of the Communion (e.g. of the Anglican Consultative Council or Lambeth) is not due to a problem of language. It is the sheer difference of the speed of life in which we live and to which we get accustomed. 'To me trying to participate in group discussions was like a ping pong game at first. The ball was too fast,' said an unhappy participant. 'Or it was like the Pool of Siloam. Each time I wanted to jump in, someone else was in there! In the end I just kept quiet.' The reverse of this is also true. I have also seen people from industrialised, high-tech countries completely out of their depth in a third-world situation. The 'local time' concept observed in respect of appointments and engagements and the leisurely way in which people tend to go about doing things frustrate and irritate the visitor. In another situation, I recall the incident regarding an ambassador who had befriended some people in a remote part of an overseas post to which he had been just assigned. On a familiarisation visit to the village, he and his wife had been so warmly welcomed that they extended an invitation to their new friends to come and see them at their home in the city. A few weeks later, in the middle of a very busy period at the Embassy, a delegation arrived from the village to spend the day, as the ambassador and his wife had done when they visited! Do we really mean it when we say, 'Drop in anytime'? What do we understand by return hospitality in certain contexts?

Culture Shock

Do we take cross-cultural differences or culture shock seriously enough? Do we try to prepare adequately? The toughest part of a conference or study or work tour in another place is half-way through. You think it will never end. The excitement brought about by novelty has worn off and the self is longing for the familiar, which brings about a sense of security and contentment. 'What am I doing in this dump, so far from home and my family?' exclaimed a very unhappy lady delegate in the middle of a

Conference in an African Province on one occasion. The expression, 'like a fish out of water,' must bring certain memories to most of us. Not understanding the game and being unable to cope, especially when one is independent and used to coping, leading and advising, can be very frustrating.

Some missionary agencies are finding it very discouraging to face the number of cases regarding missionaries they sponsor 'to go overseas' who do not settle and have to be recalled. This is always distressing for all parties concerned; a sense of failure seems to prevail. The period of training and preparation before venturing out does not seem to have been adequate. More and more there is a growing belief that a preliminary visit to the receptor diocese or church would be very beneficial, though, no doubt, costly. Cannot part of the training and preparation be done in the place of the future posting itself?

As a result of Haley's book *Roots*, a number of Americans of African origin went to the 'root' country of their ancestors before their journey across the Atlantic, with the view to settling down 'back home' if possible. The reality of things in terms of cultural and other fundamental differences soon dampened the enthusiasm of their well-meant patriotic intentions. The Rastafarians also discovered that the Promised Land of Ethiopia was a different reality from that of their dream back in the palm-fringed, multi-racial islands of Jamaica or Barbados and the rhythmic sound of the reggae.

Cultural Interaction

The interaction of the Church in one cultural form with another culture should bring about a change in outlook and lifestyle for both parties to the interaction.[13]

Is this meant to be true of the interaction of the Church only or also of the secular scene? Too often what we do witness is the attempt of one dominant culture trying to sublimate another. Values and criteria for assessing values have too much been based on formal education, technological and scientific achievements, and material wealth. Countries and nations that are economically poor may be humanly and aesthetically rich. Wealthy countries and nations sometimes contain widespread human misery.

In the midst of highly developed, industrialised countries we sometimes see indigenous peoples living as aliens and third-class citizens in their own land. Their way of life and inherited culture are regarded as outmoded and of no national importance or significance. Tensions usually build up when the land and other inheritance they claim is under threat of being taken over for industrial purposes or other forms of material development. Indigenous peoples see things another way. Their long years of experience and cultural evolution, previously undisturbed by settlers from other cultures, have brought them acquired wisdom and a love and respect for nature, with which they have become one.

Immigrants

It is of late that the receptor countries and nations have been taking serious account of the cultural and other human needs of immigrants in their midst to facilitate the process of adaptation and integration. There is a whole wealth of untapped cultural resources in many a parish or diocese with immigrant groups. From the 'threat' which the presence of such persons was feared to bring—drainage on local resources, services, job opportunities, housing and schools, loud music, highly spiced cooking, fear of courtship and intermarriage—some communities have been learning how to draw from these new human resources for the enrichment of the whole. Mixed choirs, servers, parish groups, parish church councils and representatives from the 'settlers' is no longer a novelty in some parishes and dioceses. The need for letters of introduction to the receptor incumbent and parishes cannot be over-emphasised. Too often parishioners who used to be committed and active in their home parishes often fall into anonymity and inactivity spiritually when they emigrate. In reverse, we know of expatriates from developed countries serving elsewhere who give welcome assistance and contribute to the life of the local church where they reside.

Companionship Links and Exchanges

Theological institutions could look seriously into exploring more opportunities for cross-cultural training and attachments both at the staff and student levels. The joint scheme for cross-cultural training being developed at Selly Oak, Birmingham, between the Church Missionary Society and the United Society for the Propagation of the Gospel in the United Kingdom is very commendable. As fellow Christians in developing countries seek ways of sharing with their counterparts in the North, the possibility of exchange of clergy for short or long terms also needs to be explored. A priest seconded to a parish with a large migrant population from his own homeland could assist in ministering in that parish for a while, helping to build contacts and bring new cultural insights to the receptor incumbent and his parish. The development of organised companionship links and exchanges between parishes, dioceses and provinces is also proving very enriching mutually, often with heavy doses of culture shock at the outset as movements from one culture to another take place. *The untapped possibilities are enormous.*

Culture and Youth

The International Youth Conference, the first of its kind in the Communion, held in Ireland in 1987 brought out some very encouraging and positive results. There is a need to study the new international youth culture of our day. Through their lyrics and music, their art and literature, their fashion and language, they are communicating their message to the rest of society. Can adults interpret what they are saying? The youth have reminded us that they are not the Church of tomorrow but very much part of *today's* Church itself.

Refugees

Among those marginalised by society and government, and for whom the compassionate mission of Jesus Christ needs special focusing, are refugees and immigrants. The former generally suffer from loss of identity, respect, community and hope, while the latter too frequently are forced to leave culture, country and native language behind.[14]

Very often there is a concerted effort to feed, provide shelter and medical care for refugees and other displaced persons. What is meant to be a temporary relief programme often turns into long-term or even permanent needs. Besides trying to provide for the physical necessities of the displaced, there is an underlying silent cry from the human soul which is not heard or detected. Slavery also ignored the culture and traditions of human groups in the same way that the dispossessed of our day are in many cases being reduced to mouths and tummies and not much else, often due to the sheer number of refugees, the environment and economic constraints. Far from Zion, yearning for songs and news and the whole familiar former way of life can remain a silent longing.

Culture and Technology

Churches in developing countries can learn much here from the hard lessons those of the West have gained from their own experience of the forces that have blown across their territory. Unindustrialised nations often receive a new culture and way of life from imported modern science and technology that sweep across the nation at such a speed that it is usually very late before certain adverse transformation which has taken place is realised. The Churches in Africa, Asia, Latin America are definitely being affected in this way. Do we always know what is in 'packages' we are being offered and the effect of the long term 'fall out' that usually ensues? For instance, serving for several years on the local national board for the censoring of films, one was very much aware of the difficulty in passing certain films for public viewing because of the possible harmful effects they might have had on a society that needed more time to itself to discern what it needed and ingest or reject what it took in. The question of violence, morality and ethics, for example, depicted visually or in writing from another culture that had progressively evolved or degenerated to its present state, always poses a problem for censors. The electronics media is much more than just a form of communication. It can also violate.

> The Western Churches also need both the ancient and the newer non-western Churches to help bring about a deeper re-conversion of the soul of the West. Above all it is these Churches that can help to rekindle a passionate concern for sinners, sufferers, victims of injustice, the confused and the lost.[15]

Cultural Revolution

Independence brought about quite an awakening in the minds and thoughts of new nations. Several countries changed their names, the names of their capitals and their streets. Some African countries, such as Zaire, promulgated laws or simply encouraged their citizens to abolish Christian names. Only purely African names were to be used. Some missionaries had not only encouraged the adoption of Christian names but of European family names as well—e.g. Crowther, Johnson, Dos Santos. As one's name is the most precise assertion of one's identity, identity asks the question: who am I? Like the reformers of sixteenth-century Europe, newly independent nations, fired by national zeal and pride, were determined to leave no suspicious stones unturned. One of the biggest stones here was Christianity and all that the Churches had inherited. African culture was not wholly condemned, but a vast range of its cultural practices was considered incompatible with Christianity. In school children were taught one thing and at home they practised something else. Confusion reigned.

> Many missionaries were extremely ignorant of the societies they had come to evangelise, with an ignorance partly blameworthy, partly next to inevitable . . . Their reaction over many matters did not vary greatly. This was partly due to the theological rigidity of almost all branches of the 19th and early 20th century church, but still more was it due to the intrinsic intertwining of religion and social life characteristic of traditional Africa.[16]

Polygamy

The cultural revolution in Africa focused strongly on religion quite possibly because of the influence the churches had and the easy appearance Christianity had as a culturally alienating element. Conversion to the Christian faith was bound to bring about some deep cultural changes and challenges. One such challenge was bound to be a head-on collision with polygamy, and most African societies were traditionally fairly polygamous. Many remain so. In some countries at least 20 per cent of all Christians were assumed to be in polygamous marriage in the '70s. The refusal to baptize male polygamists could have more cruel effects than the refusal of communion to a Christian taking a second wife. The former brought about the breaking of marriage and families entered into in all good faith. Should the Churches today retreat from the position maintained by the 1888 Lambeth Conference and be willing to receive polygamists to baptism? The Lambeth Conference of 1988 adopted the following resolution on the Church and polygamy:

> This Conference upholds monogamy as God's plan, and as the ideal relationship of love between husband and wife; nevertheless recommends that a polygamist who responds to the Gospel and wishes to join the Anglican Church may be baptised and confirmed with his believing wives and children on the following conditions:
>
> 1. that the polygamist shall promise not to marry again as long as any of his wives at the time of his conversion are alive;
> 2. that the receiving of such a polygamist has the consent of the local Anglican community;
> 3. that such a polygamist shall not be compelled to put away any of his wives on account of the social deprivation they would suffer;
> 4. and recommends that Provinces where the Churches face problems of polygamy are encouraged to share information of their pastoral approach to Christians who become polygamists so that the most appropriate way of disciplining and pastoring them can be found, and that the ACC be requested to facilitate the sharing of that information.[17]

Discussion on polygamy draws our attention to the need to consider other forms of human relationships in vogue among Christians. For instance, what does the Church think of polygamy by rotation—i.e. marriage, divorce, and remarriage in succession? of concubinage and trial marriages, both of which are getting quite fashionable? of marriage to non-Christians, and the religious, cultural and social implications?

Churchmanship

A subject not usually discussed in considering culture and mission is churchmanship, an inheritance from the 'Mother Churches' which tended to draw new converts into camps, sometimes resulting in the same intensity of passion based on allegiance as tribal loyalty claimed. When the theological and other relevant undergirdings of each aspect of churchmanship have been examined and positions based on personal convictions have been adopted, whatever else that has been embraced needs to be examined to sort out what affirms and enriches from appendages which are irrelevant or contrary to one's cultural enrichment and spiritual growth.

Culture and the Ministry of Women

In some cultures the traditional role of women in the family and in society is such that drastic adjustments are called for in the light of our present understanding of the biblical teaching on the ministry of all God's people, male and female. This is a very sensitive area that calls for care and understanding in order to bring about effective change. 'In our tradition, women don't even sit with their husbands for meals. They wait on their husbands. So how do you think our people will respond to the idea of women becoming pastors, presiding at the Eucharist, chairing parish meetings? Women in our diocese don't even read in church!' Are these familiar words or do they shock the ears? This is a reality which time, understanding and grace will resolve as we learn from one another and allow the Gospel to speak to our different situations.

Culture and Language

At all international meetings, the languages used are European, mostly due to the impact of European culture on the developing world during the colonial period. In the Anglican Communion and in the World Council of Churches, the majority of members do not have European languages as their mother tongue; however, these are the languages which are used. The attempts made in recent years to provide simultaneous translation at international meetings is most welcome. The task of translating relevant documents for the Decade and other needs into the vernacular is an urgent one.

The fact that Jesus spoke Aramaic is very significant. Language learning is a necessity for all missionaries if they are to be able to communicate with those among where they will live and work.

96

It is gratifying to note that over 150 years ago two Welsh missionaries, for example, were the first to put Malagasy into a written form and proceeded to produce the first translation of the Bible in that language. The Word of God in the language of any nation or tribe has proved to be one of the most powerful forms of cultural liberation and spiritual enrichment known.

Silent Language

In every culture there is also a silent language. This is most difficult to teach. It has to do with sensitivity, learning to interpret words not spoken, feelings not expressed, requests not made. It is a question of listening with the heart to hear what is 'blowing in the wind'. Prayer does much to help us tune in to and unravel the silent language of every culture and nation. One's acceptance or otherwise and one's ability to cope with a different culture often depends to a large extent on one's ability to interpret and respond to what the ears cannot hear and the eyes cannot see.

Conclusion

In 1988 we went to the Lambeth Conference as bishops of the Anglican Communion, most of us accompanied by our wives (we shall have to say 'spouses' in future) taking our dioceses with us to Canterbury. We returned home with the Decade of Evangelism. Since then, faxes, jets, boats, lorries, bicycles, horses, camels and feet have carried the Lambeth resolution to every corner of the globe.

Although when we meet as international or regional groups we usually use a European language to communicate, on home ground we invariably utilise the vernacular. As the bearers of the message of the resolution travel, they are dressed in suits, in sarongs, blankets, loin cloths or grass skirts. The leaders operate from a massive air-conditioned sky-scraper, with a host of the latest electronic apparatus around him or her, or in a hot little office with a tin or thatched roof, frequently visited by mosquitoes, alone, with an old typewriter, which he works with two fingers. Those who reflect on the resolution and praise the God who calls his Church to mission sit in large spacious buildings on comfortable chairs or under trees in open spaces.

Often, the latter do not have any printed material and have to memorise everything.

When all those who subscribe to the resolution meet for prayer or worship, a printed cycle covering all the dioceses of the Anglican Communion upholds all the situations mentioned above. And the Family Prayer, given by the One who said 'Go into all the world', is said in every conceivable tongue forming part of the worldwise family, his Church.

Culture must continue to play a very important part in writing the script, finding the music, designing the dress, interpreting the feeling, making the proclamation and attending to all the other needs of the Decade and beyond. However, 'the gospel endorses an immensely wide diversity among human cultures, but it does not endorse total relativism'.[18] Bishop Lesslie Newbigin's statement needs to be pondered over deeply.

Like lanes and roads from the outskirts of a city all converging towards it like webs around a spider, there is much in scripture that points towards the culmination of the created order as an ingathering of all the nations in a rich, harmonious multi-racial, multi-cultural celebration. Peter's vision of the sheet let down from heaven containing every living creature, every one of which was to be considered clean, was a message to the infant Church of the inconceivable harvest the centuries and millenia would bring. Many of the parables Jesus taught ended with a concept of feasting at the end, gathered around a common table, around a fatherly or kindly figure. The worship of the Lamb in Revelation says it all in more explicit language. In our own day, this is how Bishop Richard Holloway expresses the same scene in *A New Heaven*, as seen in a young man's dream:

> Nothing, it seemed, could be kept out of that radiant circle. It extended to the horizon, a great multitude which no man could number, from every nation, from all tribes and people and tongues, each praising the Lamb of God according to the manner of the knowledge given unto him. And soon the grass and the stones and the birds in flight were crying out to that centre where stood the lamb slain from the foundation of the world. And then he saw that all creation revolved round that strange centre, each thing was held in that mysterious orbit no matter how furiously it plunged away into space. Finally, he saw the whole Universe, every immeasurable

fraction of it; all of time, and the vast reaches of the ages; and he saw all struggle and loss, every wound and battle tumult; all separation and going down into dust was there; and he saw every leaf that ever was, and all love and the singing of it; beauty there was, and failure, and every road not taken; each heart-stopping moment since the foundation of the earth, held together at last in one colossal shout of praise, the great and final Amen of a transfigured creation: 'Amen. Blessing and glory and wisdom and thanksgiving and honour and power and might be to our God for ever and ever. Amen.[19]

I find that the following short litany sums up what I have been trying to say:

A Litany of Thanksgiving

We are the scattered children of Canterbury, gathered from every colour, tribe and tongue.

We give thanks for our common heritage, for the traditions of worship and order we share, for the stories of yesterday which have become part of our story today.

Response: **We praise you, O God. May we be faithful to our heritage.**

We give thanks for the glorious tapestry of cultures and worship which we weave together; for the gifts of beauty and of truth we offer to each other; for the sense that our unity in Christ is a harmony of rich diversity in which we all give and receive.

Response: **We praise you, O Christ. May we see your face, and know your grace, in one another.**

We give thanks for the deep conviction that God is not finished with us yet, that in his purpose of unity for his whole creation we are given our place and our mission.

Response: **We praise you, O Holy Spirit. May we have the courage to follow wherever you lead. Amen.'[20]**

Notes

1. Ruth 1.16,17b.
2. Matt. 1.5-6.
3. *Many Gifts One Spirit*, Report of ACC-7, 1987, p. 61.
4. *Gathered for Life*, Official Report—Sixth Assembly of WCC, 1983, p. 32.
5. Adrian Hastings, *African Christianity*, Camelot Press Ltd, p. 44.
6. John 20.21.

7. *Crossroads are for Meeting*, edited by Philip Turner and Frank Sugeno, SPCK/USA, p. 243.
8. Mark 7.24-30.
9. Acts 15.19-20.
10. *Gathered for Life*, pp. 33-34.
11. The Full Report of the Pre-Lambeth Conference for Africa, July 1987, p. 14.
12. *The Truth Shall Make You Free. The Lambeth Conference* 1988. p. 219.
13. *Many Gifts One Spirit*, p. 62.
14. Lambeth Conference 1988 Report, p. 38.
15. Ibid., p. 36.
16. *African Christianity*, p. 38.
17. Lambeth Conference 1988 Report, pp. 220-221.
18. Lesslie Newbigin, *The Gospel in a Pluralist Society*, SPCK, p. 197.
19. Richard Holloway, *A New Heaven*, Mowbrays, pp. 124-125.
20. *Mission in a Broken World*, Report of ACC-8, 1990, p. 111.

7

CONTEXT OF PEOPLE OF GOD IN COMMUNITY

Jaci Maraschin

I

The people of God do not live only in the context of the people of God. Perhaps we should ask at the outset if it is proper to speak of a concept of the people of God? Can the concepts of 'context' and 'people of God' be put together in our present situation? To make things a little more difficult we have also the concept of 'community'. Where do the people of God experience community, and in which context? The three realities we are talking about have to be seen against the background of a larger statement, which is the 'sharing of good news through mission'. And all this has to be discussed and interpreted having in mind the ecumenical decade of evangelism.

1. I will start this reflection with some remarks on the three concepts put together in the title of this chapter. Let us, then, start with the word 'context'. This word became very important in Third World theological circles through the efforts of the contemporary ecumenical movement. Indeed, the Theological Education Fund[1] of the World Council of Churches, in the 1970s, transformed it into the key concept for a memorable programme of theological education related to the Third World in particular, but never excluding the First World.[2] The derived word 'contextualization' came to mean the effort to relate theological education to the local or regional situations in which that education was being done. This was also related to former theological perspectives of the same World Council of Churches, well expressed through slogans like 'the World provides the agenda'. The context, which meant the social, cultural, economic and political situation, became a sort of a first pole in a bipolarity consisting of 'context and gospel'.[3] Theology became liberal again. We should start from the context and not from the Gospel. We

should avoid the radicality of Karl Barth in his earliest writings, and try to build a bridge between the world and the gospel. Tillich's advice sounded better: the church should listen to the questions implicit in the situation before trying to deliver the good news of the gospel or, in the theme of our book, before 'sharing the good news through mission'.[4] In a way, Latin American Theology of Liberation tried to do this with seriousness and depth. But this theology, born out of our poverty and oppression, was too much on the side of the 'context' to be sufficiently radical to criticize itself and its methodology. We should not blame our Latin American theologians. They had the enthusiasm of youth, the commitment to the people, and the energy to fight against injustice. The pole of 'context' had to be overwhelming and imposing. This was beautiful and full of life. But now, after more than twenty years, we in Latin America are returning to the radical protest of our faith and applying it not only to our context but also to our theology.

2. The concept of 'people of God' is a very powerful and explosive one. If we apply this concept to the organized church it will explode not the church but the institutional organization of the church. We use the concept in a very loose way because we are afraid of the effect of its use. If the church is 'the people of God' it cannot be simply the bishops of God. Symbols are decisive elements in the life of the church and the world. If the church is really 'the people of God' it should never be called 'Episcopal'. It is slightly heretical to use this word to name the community of the people of God. We are so used to this that we do not even think about it. I was reading the June 1991 issue of *Compasrose*,[5] which carries the news of the Anglican Communion all over the world and was very interested in the section on 'people'. The eighteen people listed in that section were all bishops. Most of them were newly elected bishops or newly consecrated bishops. Some of them were bishops changing positions or receiving honours of some kind. It seems that we can only be people of God if we became bishops. The concept of people of God transcends the ecclesiastical boundaries. This is why I found it so difficult to speak of a proper 'context of people of God'. They live in the larger context of the world and they are women and men of all sorts and conditions, of all races and ages, and the only sign to make this people of God visible is the radical

allegiance they show to Jesus, as the Christ, in whatever context they live.

3. Though the concept of 'community' has been studied especially in sociology, the best expression of it is found in the Book of Acts:

> They devoted themselves to the apostles' teaching and fellowship, to the breaking of the bread and the prayers. Awe came upon everyone, because many wonders and signs were being done by the apostles. All who believed were together and had all things in common; they would sell their possessions and goods and distribute the proceeds to all, as any had need. Day by day, as they spent much time together in the temple, they broke bread at home and ate their food with glad and generous hearts, praising God and having the good-will of all the people. And day by day the Lord added to their number those who were being saved. (Acts 2. 44-47)

This was the experience of community for the people of God. The meaning of community depended on that experience. And this is still the meaning of community for the same people of God in our day. This community seems to us completely out of context. In that situation it could not fit harmoniously into the structure of the temple. It had to create its own context, though it was much more like a promise than a factual reality. It had the substance of a utopia. Its life was marked by two poles: the temple and the houses. They pointed to the limits of a context. On the other hand, the temple and the houses belonged to a wider context which was tradition, society, economy and the political life. The community 'spent much time together in the temple'. The meaning of this togetherness 'in the temple' signifies, perhaps, a common protest in face of the wider context in which the temple would be seen as not only the house of God but also the meeting of common interests of the people, not always according to the law of love, but to the law of the market, far away from the worship of the true God. We should remember that Jesus criticised the temple transformed into a market place: 'In the temple he found people selling cattle, sheep and doves, and the money changers seated at their tables', and 'he drove all of them out of the temple'[7] But it was in the houses that they lived their community life breaking bread and eating. Community life was above the temple and above the houses, though they never denied the place the temple and the houses had in their lives. In order to have community in the wider context of society and tradition, the people of God had to judge them according to the higher principle of the gospel and, of course, the Word of God. Their attitude demonstrated that the temple was an ambiguous place. They would go together into the temple but would not break the bread nor eat in the temple. Also, in the same measure as they despised the sense of property linked to houses and other goods, they had to live in houses and have their own goods. But they learned to criticise them in order to see the kingdom of God beyond possessions and goods. They would use them but would not put in them their trust and hope. So, the life of the people of God in community represented a new vision of the temple and of the houses. This was a life of common sharing.

II

I move now into another kind of interpretation. If it is true that there was not a context of the people of God but a general context which they criticised while living in its boundaries, we should look at that context in the light of the meaning of 'people of God in community'. I will try to examine this question under four propositions: (1) the general context was a complex of pride and certainties, not of humility; (2) it was traditional and, therefore, willing to preserve laws, rules and institutions instead of trans-forming them: it lacked imagination; (3) it was dominated by the shallowness and emptiness of daily affairs and interests: it lacked beauty; (4) in that context life was heavy and difficult: it lacked lightness.

1. The sharing of the good news of the gospel in mission happens in a context of bad news. From the first century until today the context, *mutatis mutandis*, is the same. The imperialism of the first centuries had a different form, of course, but the essence of it was the same. Imperialism is a state of affairs experienced through history with different names. At the time of the primitive church it was manifest in the Roman imperial state. In modern times it has taken different forms from Nazism, Fascism, Stalinism to the creation of the new hegemony of the North Atlantic countries in Europe and in America. In our days the so-called democratic nations announce freedom and prosper-

ity around the world but act in a diverse and contradictory way. Theology of Liberation in Latin America has criticised the capitalist system on the grounds of its pride and sense of superiority. We are aware that the failure of socialism in Eastern Europe does not represent the victory of capitalism. Capitalism may, perhaps, have some success for some people in comparatively very few places in the world. It has not been able to create freedom for everyone nor prosperity or health. The capitalist world may have a dozen fairly nice and prosperous countries surrounded by a sea of hundreds of Third World countries facing misery, oppression, domination, all sorts of exploitation and diseases. So what should be the 'sharing of good news in mission' in such a worldwide context?

Christians are called to announce a message that cannot be compromised with any other message we hear through the electronic media or through the many 'saviours of this world'. The Christian message is, in itself, a protest against all the easy offers of salvation presented in the windows of political parties, religious societies, methods of self-salvation, magic rites or witchcraft. Though we have to live in the wider context of capitalism we cannot praise capitalism. The message of the free market is not our message. We may stand together 'in the temple' and may hold properties, 'breaking bread' and 'eating together', as pilgrims. The context of people of God in community is a context of protest in face of the wider context of society. This protest takes the form of humility. In a society having wealth as its God, Christians choose voluntary poverty as their road to God. (Cf. John 2. 14-15).

We read in the gospels:

> No one can serve two masters; for a slave will either hate the one and love the other, or be devoted to the one and despise the other. You cannot serve God and wealth. (Matt. 6.24)

This means, naturally, that the sharing of good news in mission in our capitalist context means to take the side of the poor and humble. They are the blessed ones. (Matt. 5.3,5). Theology of Liberation has been insisting on the preferential option for the poor and this is not a mere fad nor a leftist political programme. It comes from the heart of the gospel. It is helpful in this context to return to one of the best known neo-orthodox theologians of our century. Karl Barth, trying to understand his position in relationship to the poor and the oppressed. Commenting on the mercy and righteousness of God he says:

> . . . it is important to notice that the people to whom God in his righteousness turns as helper and Saviour is everywhere in the Old Testament harassed and oppressed people of Israel, which, powerless in itself, has no rights, and is delivered over to the superior force of its enemies; and in Israel it is especially the poor, the widows and orphans, the weak and defenceless.

The option for the poor does not come from any political or philosophical ideology but from the love of God manifest in Christ. We have to insist on this point especially when liberation theologians are threatened by the wider context of our world and by ecclesiastical authorities submissive to that context. But this option was not the creation of Gustavo Gutierrez and his friends in Latin America. It comes from the Bible. The perception that God takes sides was very strong in Barth also.

> . . . the human righteousness required by God . . . has necessarily the character of a vindication of right in favour of the threatened innocent, the oppressed poor, widows, orphans and aliens. For this reason, in the relations and events in the life of his people, God always takes his stand unconditionally and passionately on this side and on this side alone: against the lofty and on behalf of the lowly; against those who already enjoy right and privilege and on behalf of those who are denied it and deprived of it.[7]

One of the clearest texts of the New Testament on the love of God for the poor and oppressed people comes from the wonderful story of Mary, the mother of Jesus. In her well-known song, the Magnificat, she proclaims in a most beautiful way the preference of God for the poor:

> He has brought down the powerful from their thrones and lifted the lowly;
> He has filled the hungry with good things and sent the rich away empty. (Luke 1. 52-53)

But more important than this, in this song, is the subversion expressed in the second verse:

He has looked with favour on the lowliness of his servant. (Luke 1. 48)

The proud he has scattered: And the proud were always the powerful, the rich, and they were all men. Not that all men were proud and all women humble. But by the influence of society they were the leaders and had accepted the evil structure of patriarchy with the correspondent submission of women to men. The case of Mary is, whatever else it might be, a protest against the pride of patriarchalism and the elevation of women to the condition of freedom and justice. She was aware of her lowliness. But she was also aware of the great things the Lord was doing for her. We should not be misled by the miraculous element in the narrative of the virgin birth. We are tempted by our patriarchal heritage to see in it only the action of the Holy Spirit on behalf of the generation of the child. But we miss the point when we are unable also to see in the story the preference of God for the humble and meek, and God's judgement on the proud and the powerful, especially on men. The Spirit was working to bring a new life into the world through that woman; and she was going to be blessed throughout all generations. Maternity was released from the bondage of patriarchalism as, on the other hand, sex was also released from its solely procreative purposes.

When we are trying to share the good news in mission we have to give attention to the poor and the lowly. The poor and the lowly are the hungry, the oppressed and the starving. But the lowly are also the women in our patriarchal society. We know who the oppressed are. They are many and their names would make a long list. But in this decade of evangelism we are also celebrating another decade: the decade of the church in solidarity with women. Are we ready not only to make a general option for the poor and the oppressed, but also join our sisters in their struggle for liberation in the church and in the world?

2. *The general context was and is traditional, and, therefore, willing to preserve laws, rules and institutions instead of transforming them: it lacked and still lacks imagination.*

We live by tradition, inside a tradition, and tend to perpetuate that tradition. Any tradition creates laws and institutions. It becomes a model to be followed by all. Indeed, laws and institutions are the basic framework of tradition. Our context is our tradition. We tend to keep our tradition. We are afraid of losing its power. Tradition is always threatened by other traditions, and in order to secure the values of our tradition we build safeguards around it. Traditions are born out of imagination but in the long run they lose the capacity for imagining. Imagination relates to image.

According to Genesis human beings were created in the image and likeness of God ('Let us make humankind in our image, according to our likeness'). This image was inclusive. It was male and female. Th original word *tzélém* means something like a sculpture and *demût* (likeness) is a sort of interpretation of *tzélém*. Von Rad points to the fact that the two concepts were related to the human being as a whole, spirit and body.[8] No wonder that the religion of the Old Testament developed a strong anthropocentric bias, even if the rest of creation could be seen as good and splendid as human beings were. Theologians have accepted the Genesis concept of image of God too easily and too quickly, to start from it a tradition hardly criticised or changeable. Because God in the Bible is never presented as image, as *tzélém*, it becomes very difficult to understand how a non-imaginable God could create imaginable human beings 'in his image and likeness'. This may be the reason why tradition tried to spiritualise that image, taking out of the image that which was imaginable. But if the body is part of the image, and indeed there is no reason why it should not be, then nature as a whole, which is also imaginable, should be part of God's image at least in the sense in which to create is to imagine. The same root for image in Greek applies also to idol and to idea. Imagination is creativity in the sense in which it is also that which we think. But thinking in our tradition was much more related to words than to images, and Christian tradition became through the centuries subservient to the tradition of words, of speaking, of arguing, and easily turned into apologetics. Luther was so radically bound by words that he once wrote: 'The ears are the only organs of a Christian'.[9]

From the Greeks to the present day, Western tradition has been logocentric. Jacques Derrida has denounced our context for what he calls 'deconstruction'. Thomas McCarthy, in a very lucid study on Derrida's thinking, explains that:

> Derrida's deconstructionism is generally perceived to be a critical, even sceptical enterprise—a perception nurtured, no doubt, by his characterisations of it. To deconstruct, he has told us, is to 'desediment', 'destabilise', 'uproot', and 'overturn' inherited concepts and schemes, 'to turn them against their own presuppositions', to 'loosen', 'undo', 'decompose', and 'dismantle' them.[10]

Why do that? Precisely because logocentrism became an idol; we were taught to consider certain confusions as truth, written documents as reliable sources of history, and ancient texts as written by the gods. According to Derrida there is a *difference* between the written text and the reality behind it. This difference is what really matters, if any thing matters at all. From what I am able to understand from Derrida's writings, the difference is not present in words. Words at the most may show its absence. This is one of the traits of post-modern thinking and acting. Traditions are mostly documents. They survive through books. And the books are for reading. This is why our chief organ is the ear. How can we deconstruct all that in the name of our good news of the gospel to be shared today? Is the good news of the gospel the *trans*mission of a *tra*dition? The context of people of God in community must be different from the context of people of God in a book. Community is not a book. It is not merely a written reality. It is not a catechism.

Following from the insights of deconstruction, but not exactly following deconstructionism, we should now turn to the concept of image as central to our missionary work. And image has to do with liturgy, with feelings and memories. To imagine means to create. Let us think of an imaginative God, the creator of the universe, in a wider context than the limited anthropocentrism brought to us by our logocentric tradition. Then perhaps, we may have hope to develop new theologies for mission which will consider seriously the human body, nature in general and ecology in particular.

3. *The general context was and is dominated by the shallowness and emptiness of daily affairs and interests: it lacked and still lacks beauty.*

An imaginative theology will necessarily be interested in forms. If it wants to be a trans*form*ing theology *form* should be a primary element in its making. Form has always been related to creation and imagination. God not only imagined his creation but also formed it. The Genesis narrative shows God as an artisan. 'Then the Lord God *formed* man from the dust of the ground'. He works surprisingly. Takes a rib from his creature and 'the rib that the Lord God had taken from the man he made into a woman . . .' There is a delightful atmosphere around this primeval workshop. The result of such a joyous work was beauty. Beauty and goodness, almost as synonymous, are related in the creative process. God enjoyed his creation and took pleasure in the contemplation of it. Beauty was from the beginning a revelation, the disclosing of something new, the appearance of the world.

One of the best modern interpretations of the work of art (was not the creation of the world a work of art?) can be found in Heidegger's *Holzwege*. Like the world, the work of art speaks and reveals and conceals truth at the same time. Heidegger says: 'Beauty is a way that truth as unconcealment happens',[11] And truth is for him nothing else than revelation. Truth is not something that can be apprehended by our intellectual faculty, but it is like a happening. It belongs much more to the world of imagination than to logocentrism. The *form* of the work of art expresses the tension existing between the earth (our mother) and the 'world'. I am trying to say that the *form* of the work expresses that tension. This tension exists in itself. It is not derived from something else. It is not a copy, like copies of real things painted by some painters through many periods of history. That is why I say it *exists*.

The world is the wider context in which we live. The earth is the source and foundation of any context possible. There is no copy in this tension. It exists. It is like the world created. God was not copying from any other source beyond his own imagination. This sense of the aesthetic leads us into contemplation. And contemplation does not require from us the use of a special rational faculty or of any kind of logic.

The general context of our world has transformed the work of art into a shallow experience of the same. Instead of the uniqueness of the artistic experience we have repetition as the basic phenomenon of our days. We are unable to see the thing as it is in its appearance. We are tempted to ask for its meaning. The philosopher Walter Benjamin spent some time trying to study what has happened to art in our modern world. Art, according to him, had 'an aura' making it unique and irrepeatable. The contemporary mass media and the printing industry have destroyed this aura and ugliness took the place of beauty. Then the context became also ugly. Vision is unable to see, and our ears, as in the time of Jesus, cannot listen any more.

For Jesus, nature was the most beautiful of any work made by human hands:

> Look at the birds of the air ... why do you worry about clothing? Consider the lilies of the field, how they grow ... yet I tell you, even Solomon in all his glory was not clothed like one of these. (Matt.6. 26,28,29)

Yes, we have now the industry of plastic and we 'adorn' our houses with plastic. Plastic figures are made in series and they have no depth nor life. Very few pictures are of good quality. In general they follow the shallowness of modern life and repeat the same story, the same models. The shallowness of our work reflects the shallowness of life in our big cities, full of pollution and dirt. Nothing inside. Like the Pharisees of Jesus' time:

> Woe to you, scribes and Pharisees, hypocrites! For you clean the outside of the cup and of the plate, but inside they are full of greed and self-indulgence. You blind Pharisee! First clean the inside of the cup, so that the outside also may become clean ... for you are like whitewashed tombs, which on the outside look beautiful, but inside they are full of the bones of the dead and of all kinds of filth. (Matt.23. 25-27)

Like the 'hollow men' of T. S. Eliot.

In the midst of this sad context of ugliness 'Jesus took with him Peter and James and his brother John and led them up a high mountain, by themselves. And he was transfigured before them, and his face shone like the sun, and his clothes became dazzling white ... Peter said to Jesus, 'Lord, it is good for us to be here' (Matt.7. 1,2,4)

How can we share the good news of the gospel in mission in the context of shallowness and emptiness? The church cannot present a word without imagination. The liturgy of the church participates also in that repetitious shallowness and much of our discourse does not go beyond the logocentric tradition of our Western civilization. How can we reject the emptiness of our social life, of our small gatherings, of our small talk in everyday life?

Our life in community can take the form of a protest in face of the hollow context in which we have to live. Community life is like a work of art. It can reveal the depth of life or it can conceal it. We may stay on the surface of experience or we can descend into its foundations and taste the joy of a new life. Jesus lived in a time of oppression and was himself the victim of political hate and persecution. He was aware of the shallowness of his own society and culture. His preaching and ministry of liberation to the poor and the needy was not always successful.

> But to what will I compare this generation? It is like children sitting in the market places and calling to one another, 'we played the flute for you, and you did not dance.' (Matt.11. 16-17)

The sharing of the good news of the gospel to the world is like this playing of the flute and this calling to dance. The context of people of God in community is the context in which this calling can be heard and this dance becomes possible.

4. *In the general context life was and still is heavy, hard and difficult: it lacked and still lacks lightness.*

Lightness was always related to air, light, angels, spiritual pleasures, art and ideas. Classical Greek philosophy had a certain distrust of matter. In *Phaedrus*, for instance, Plato develops his theory of ideas. In his fanciful mythological construction the soul is light and has wings to fly above through the heavens. Souls are guided to these high places attracted by truth. They are helped by gods and in their pilgrimage they forget the low passions. When souls are faithful to a god they are free from all evil. But when they cannot follow the gods they look for impure food, vices and fall, finally, into amnesia. Then they become heavy and fall down to the earth full of matter. Matter and the body are heavy entities and represent a deviation of the original purpose of creation. Plato embellished his theory with imagination and literary skill to accentuate the fundamental idea that originally the soul was free of any stain and had no body. The body, then, represented the prison of the soul. This was a very strong idea that through Neoplatonism influenced the Christian Church from the beginning until today. Of course, heaviness was not always a negative concept for the majority of philosophers. Descartes, for instance, equated the possibility of knowledge to the weighty and measurable character of matter. On the other hand, weightiness was always related to hard labour, and the most difficult physical tasks were left to slaves and workers belonging to the lower classes of society.

The concept of heaviness, applied always in general to hard matter and to the human body in particular, affected our understanding of the material world and is responsible for a tradition suspicious of everything sensible and bodily. Very early in the life of the Church sin inhabited the body and from there attacked the soul, always fragile and in danger of being seduced.

These few remarks are only introductory to the new meaning of heaviness and lightness in the modern world. Both concepts may relate to action, duties and social manifestations in our societies.

We are not much concerned about heavy matter nor about the weight of our bodies. Heaviness became a spiritual concept with the connotation of everything (spiritual as well as material) which represents a hindrance to the realisation of our human destiny. So, slavery is weighty, and freedom light. Ugliness is heavy and beauty is light. Pride and certainties are heavy: humility is light.

When we look at the general context of the world this is a heavy and hard world. Jesus spoke about the hardness of human hearts. The system of competition brought about by the law of the free market makes human relationships hard and weighty. Our social institutions put on us heavy burdens, as did the scribes and the Pharisees in Jesus' time. This is the principal reason for the denunciation of Jesus:

> Jesus said to the crowds and to the disciples: 'The scribes and the Pharisees sit on Moses's seat; therefore, do whatever they teach you and follow it; but do not do as they do, for they do nor practise what they teach. They tie up heavy burdens, hard to bear, and lay them on the shoulders of others; but they themselves are unwilling to lift a finger to move them.' (Matt. 23. 1-4)

This is like the war situation in our contemporary world. The chief of the nations are like the scribes and Pharisees. They call soldiers and they impose on them heavy burdens hard to bear, the worst of all being the killing of the supposed enemies and the destruction of towns and cities. The most powerful nations make war far away from their own land. But the chief of these nations 'are unwilling to lift a finger' to bring into action their deadly missiles.

We live in a world tired of racism, sexism and all sorts of discrimination against the lowly and the poor. They are heavy burdens to be carried along the way. The sharing of the good news of the gospel has to be a denunciation of all the heavy burdens. It has to be a message of lightness.

> Jesus said: 'Come to me, all you that are weary and are carrying heavy burdens, and I will give you rest. Take my yoke upon you, and learn from me; for I am gentle and humble in heart, and you will find rest for your souls. For my yoke is easy and my burden is light.' (Matt.11. 28-30)

This is the lightness of the gospel. In a context of heavy burdens and violence, the good news of the gospel can only be the announcing of the possibility of a new context of lightness. The context of the world is not the context of the people of God. If the primitive Church could say without hesitation that Christ's Kingdom was not of this world the meaning was not a calling to retreat but to protest. The kingdom of this world is a kingdom of pride, tradition, shallowness and heaviness. The Kingdom of God is a kingdom of love expressed through humility, freedom, beauty and lightness.

III

Postscript

The mission of the Church is unique. Its uniqueness makes it important and relevant in face of the world. But the relevance of the mission of the Church is not the same relevance as that of agencies of social action or of effective political parties. The mission of the Church is not relevant in that sense. The mission of the Church does not aim at bringing a new social order to the world. It is not a programme of building better and cheaper houses for the poor or even of starting the revolutions we would like to sponsor. In this sense the mission of the Church is irrelevant and rightly so.

1. In the long history of missions the Church was haunted many times by a triumphalist enthusiasm and took as model not the Kingdom of God but the Roman Empire. It made alliances with kings and emperors and was happy when it arrived at the condition of a State Church. The ministry, which was humble and simple in the days of Jesus, followed the imperialist model, and instead of humility it was proud and full of worldly splendours. Nothing was more logical from the human point of view than to preserve the inherited privileges and interpret them as necessary for the preservation of its life and message. This is why our discourses became contradictory. Should we, then, change the discourse to fit our structure or, rather, change the structure in order to fit the discourse? Do we need a new reformation in order to be truthful to the mission?

2. We have much to preserve from the past. But the model for mission cannot be the preservation of the past. Missionary activity cannot be the mere repetition of nineteenth-century theology and practices. Some of our missionary societies still work like that. They send their foreign missionaries to repeat among our native peoples that which was and still may be good for England or America. What we need in our Third World countries is not the camouflaged transplantation of alien cultures in the name of the Gospel, but a partnership able to rediscover the meaning of mission in an unprecedented way. It seems that some of our missionary societies lack imagination. They want to preserve tradition. But what kind of tradition? Our native peoples have also their own traditions and they are as sacred and valuable as any other.

3. Liturgy is an important part of mission. If it should not be a pamphleteer, on the one hand, it should not only repeat old liturgical tradition, on the other. Liturgical worship has been shallow and dry in most of our churches. We should pay much more attention to the new discoveries of the liturgical movement, especially regarding music, dance, visual aids and a new sense of life in community. Liturgy and spirituality go together, and the soul of mission is, of course, the Holy Spirit. We are called to restore beauty as the leading experience of our encounter with God and with our sisters and brothers.

115

4. To be a Christian is a joyous experience. It is the experience of grace. The experience of sin is heavy and sad. The experience of grace is the experience of lightness, which is also forgiveness and transfiguration. This experience takes away all pride, because what we do does not count any more, but only what God does for us through Christ in the power of the Holy Spirit. To be a Christian means to enjoy the fruits of the Spirit: love, joy, peace, patience, kindness, generosity, faithfulness, gentleness and self-control (Gal.5.22). The fruits of the Spirit are related not only to our personal life nor only to our community life, but also to the wider context in which we have to live. The context includes the world with its pride, its traditions and false securities; its shallowness and ugliness, and its heaviness. The lightness of the Christian life is the most relevant aspect of mission because it includes all the other elements we mentioned above and in its irrelevancy represents the most profound criticism of the weightiness and dryness of our contemporary society.

The context of people of God in community has to be a context of lightness and joy. This new context contrasts vividly with the wider context of the world. It is a promising possibility of mission in our time.

Notes

1. It was later on transformed into the *Program of Theological Education.*
2. Cf. *Ministry in Context, The Third Mandate Programme of The Theological Education Fund* (1970-1977), London, TEF, 1972. Also *Learning in Context, The Search for Innovative Patterns in Theological Education,* TEF, Geneva, Switzerland, 1973.
3. Very easily the concept of context becomes interchangeable with the concept of world, with the disadvantage that the concept of world is much more extensive and complex than the former one.
4. Tillich develops this bipolarity in the Introduction of his *Systematic Theology.*
5. Partnership House, 157 Waterloo Road, London, England.
6. This expression was employed by Dr Chung in her address in Canberra for the Seventh General Assembly of the World Council of Churches in February 1991.
7. *Church Dogmatics,* II/1, Edinburgh, T & T Clark, 1957, p. 386.
8. Gerhard von Rad, *Theologie des Alten Testaments,* Christian Kaiser Verlag, 1957, II, B, 1,i.
9. *Luther's Works,* Philadelphia, Fortress Press, USA, v. 29, p. 244.

10. In *Hermeneutics and Critical Theory in Ethics and Politics*, ed. Michael Kelly, The MIT Press, USA, 1990, p. 153.
11. *Holzwege*, 4th ed, Frankfurt, Klostermann, 1963, p.44. The first essay is translated into English in *Philosophies of Art and Beauty*, ed. A. Hofstadter and Richard Kuhns. New York, Random House, 1964, p. 61.

Section III
Movement to Mission: a Massive Shift

8

TRAINING THE LAITY AND CLERGY FOR MISSION— THE ROLE OF EVERY CHRISTIAN

James Fenhagen

Not long ago I ran across a friend who at the end of a long conversation told me about an experience that he described as changing his life. My friend is a member of a parish in Connecticut, a business man, and described himself at the time as an 'average churchgoer'. He told me about how, as he was leaving a hospital where he had been visiting his mother, he met a man whom he had known casually from the parish they both attended. The man had just left the room where his wife had died after a sudden heart attack. The man was grief-stricken and distraught and was clearly crying out for help. My friend sat down with the man and listened as the man poured out his pain. As he gradually began to collect himself he said to my friend, 'I need my church' and my friend, almost without thinking, responded, 'I *am* your church' and the man reached out and took my friend's hand.

As my friend recounted the story to me, and as I recall his words, he shared what was for him a critical moment. 'When he said to me, I *need my church*, I discovered something about myself that I had never understood before. The words came tumbling out and I knew that I was for this man at this moment the presence of Jesus Christ. I was the church there in that hospital five miles away from where I worship on Sunday'. Then he went on to say that although he had heard a lot about the ministry of the laity preached about in his parish, it never took root until that moment when he suddenly understood in a new way who he was and, in some indescribable way, what his life was about.

In theological terms, what my friend was describing was a particular moment in his life when he laid claim to his baptism. No doubt the Spirit had been working at this for some time—in bits and pieces—until that moment when it all seemed to come together. Holy Baptism in the Christian Church is that sacramental action by which we are incorporated into the Body of Christ and given the gift of ministry—the gift that for most of us is claimed later as we mature and our life unfolds. This claiming of our baptismal ministry is what I believe the service of Confirmation is about and I look forward to the day when the service can be revised and administered at an age when what we are about is more clear. The authority for ministry given to us in baptism is an intrinsic authority that comes from within. I speak and act in the name of Jesus Christ because through baptism the risen Christ dwells in me and I in him. This is where the authority for ministry comes from. What the church does is confirm what has already been given—helping us to use our gifts in ways that are authentic, appropriate and helpful to others.

I have often dreamed of what it would be like if after every baptism a seat in the congregation was set aside with the name of the new Christian inscribed on it. After the child was baptized we would take her to her seat which would be hers as long as she was a part of the congregation. This would be her place and if for some reason on a given Sunday she was not present, those people on either side of her would take up her intercessions so that none of the energy of the congregation would be lost. This is what it means to be the Body of Christ gathered to share in Jesus' priestly intercession on behalf of the world—a people gathered each with a place and each with a part. I know my dream is a bit idealistic because we don't have assigned seats and as soon as many people are baptized they move away. The point, I believe, remains an important one. The claiming of our baptismal ministry has to do with place and presence. To live in Christ means to own our place in the gathered community and understand what it means to be the instrument of the presence of Jesus Christ in the church scattered—wherever this happens to be. Ministry is experienced when this sense of place and presence come together. The way we act and what we say is for us the expression of our life in Christ.

The Church Gathered and Scattered

I don't know when I first heard the words, 'gathered' and 'scattered' to describe the Christian Church in the world, but I have always found what these words represent to be extremely helpful. What lies behind these words is the image of a dynamic community of people who gather for worship where they are reconnected with the risen Christ and called to share in his priestly intercession on behalf of the world. Then they scatter into all the nooks and crannies of the world as signs and instruments of Jesus' healing presence to others. This, of course, is what life in Christ is about. It is a rhythm of gathering and scattering—of drawing in and reaching out. At the conclusion of our parish worship when the dismissal is pronounced, 'Go in peace to love and serve the Lord', with the response, 'Thanks be to God', there is a sense of immense energy, explosive energy if you will, about to be released again into those communities where the congregation came from.

This image of the local church reflects that mission oriented understanding of the church that we see described in the Book of Acts, but, unfortunately, is an image that has been lost to much of the church today. If the Decade of Evangelism proclaimed by our church does nothing more than help us realise that we are in a mission situation that is every bit as real and every bit as urgent as the one faced by the first century church, the proclamation will have been successful. We are living in a world that is not only largely unchurched, but a world that is in deep, deep pain. It is to this world that in Christ each of us is sent.

When most people think of the church I suspect they think in terms of the church gathered, with ministry emanating from this central source. Although in many cases Christian ministry does occur this way, it places the emphasis in the wrong place. When we think of Christian ministry as beginning in a church building and moving outward, there is a sense that the further away from the building we get, the less important the ministry is. Although we don't say this out loud, we imply that to be a vestry-person, or a lay reader or a priest, is more Christian than to be a Christ-bearer in a school or in an office or in a labour union or in the home. The result of such a way of thinking is that most of our energy goes into maintenance rather than mission. We take care of what really is important—the gathered church.

But for the moment let's reverse this image and see what difference it makes. Instead of looking at the church from inside out—from gathered to scattered, let's look at it the other way round—from scattered to gathered. When I think of the church this way I see first men, women and children scattered throughout the city and beyond bearing witness to the healing presence of Jesus Christ in thousands of different ways. I see a man arguing in a Board Meeting for policies that provide greater incentives for employees on the lower end of the company pay scale. I see a woman organizing young people in a housing project to reaffirm their efforts to stay away from drugs. I see a recovering alcoholic on a twelfth step visit to another man in the depths of an alcoholic despair. I see men and women serving on school boards or community action groups or visiting in hospitals or gathered together for breakfast with other Christians in Bible study and prayer. Where is the church, you say? I say, here is the church. It is a church on fire with the gospel and committed to being a healing presence in that world we are called to serve. When you look at the church this way the criteria for success is not only the number of people at worship, but the quality and variety of ministries this church supports and the impact it has on the community where it functions.

When we see the church this way, the gathered church is seen primarily as a resource for the church scattered. We gather to be fed, to be renewed, to enter into the story of our redemption and to share in Jesus' never ending prayer for the world, in order that our primary ministries might be reinforced, energised and supported. If we are to be faithful to our calling, everything we do in the church must be in the service of mission—and mission can be as straightforward and down-to-earth as one person saying to another, 'Friend, let me tell you about Jesus Christ and what he has meant in my life. Let me tell you about what he means to the world'. Certainly, one measure of the degree to which we have laid claim to our baptism is our ability to say these words or words like them to someone in need.

Problems and Possibilities

Throughout its history the Christian Church has wrestled with the image of itself as a besieged fortress surrounded by a hostile world. We even talk about Christians leaving the church building to go out into the world—as if when we entered a church building we left the world behind. The church does seek to uphold values that often differ from the values of the market place and sometimes differ in more radical ways than we want to admit but, nevertheless, there is still only one world and we all live in it whether we are in the church or out on the street.

The point is an important one. The church is not a fortress against a hostile world called secular humanism from which we send raiding parties to bring people in where they will be promised safety. It is, as the Bible suggests, more like leaven placed in the midst of the hustle and bustle of life to change values and empower relationships and to bring meaning and hope to all it touches. This means for the Christian all life is ministry, for ministry is not so much about doing a job as it is about living and the implications of our baptism. Ministry is about life in Christ which affects everything we do.

The big step every Christian has to take involves moving from a consumer mode in relation to the gathered church to a participant mode—the move from 'what does the church do for me?' to 'what do we, the church, do for the world?' When Paul speaks of the need for 'our minds to be remade and our whole natures transformed' (Rom.12.2) he is alluding to this very fundamental change in the way we see ourselves. Although I am nourished by the gathered church, it is not *they*, but *we*. I *am* the church, because Christ lives in me and I in him. It is this simple fact that describes who I am and what my life is about. I am (to put it rather simply) Jim + Jesus + you (the community of faith).

There are a lot of things in the church that make it difficult for us to claim the ministries we have been given. If you are still in a consumer mode—still hoping to find the perfect church that will solve all your problems—this ministry will always be heard as a request to take on another job in the midst of an already busy schedule. We clergy make it hard for people to claim their ministries because we only seem to give value to work done in the gathered church. Maybe it is because we find it hard to honour ministries we cannot control or because our need for help in building a strong institution becomes the driving force for our theology. Men and women complain about the lack of support or encouragement they experience for the often difficult ministries they are undertaking, and clergy complain about the unwillingness of the laity to take the risk that would bring about the transformation of which Paul speaks. I shall always remember a member of a congregation I once served saying to me that I never need expect him to join in small groups in the parish because he didn't like being personal about his religion. There are groups that have fed me and groups that haven't, but unless I am willing to share something of myself with another Christian, the chances are high that a consumer Christian I will always be—and of course, as we all know, such resistance to the Spirit who calls us into relationship with others is not limited to the laity. It is sometimes the clergy who are the least available of all.

The point, of course, is that we are all in this together. It is not *we* or *they* but *us* and if the church is to be the missionary community it is called to be, we all very much need each other. People are drawn to the church when they not only hear about nurture and caring and challenge, they experience it. The call to ministry, therefore, invites us to build up the gathered church— to care for it and to exercise ministries that strengthen it—and then to *be* that church wherever during the week I find myself. Ministry, therefore, is both a matter of *intention* and *presence*. We bring our Gospel values to the work place and bear witness when the time is right. Or we go about our day to day lives alert to the ever present cry for help which often comes when we don't expect it. What makes life a ministry of presence is that it is rooted in prayer and shaped by regular contact with the Word of God. Ministries of presence are fundamentally servant ministries, making ourselves available to others in ways that reflect the presence of Christ in our midst.

If we are serious about living out our baptism, we also need to exercise ministries of intention. When I am intentional about doing one thing in the name of Jesus Christ, it makes everything else I do more focused and more in touch with the Spirit who makes all ministry possible. For a given period of time I might discern that my gifts can best be used teaching a high school class in my gathered church on Sunday. I am called to do this because my gifts as a teacher have been confirmed by others and I recognize that the need is great. Or maybe my intentional ministry for a given period of time is to serve as the Chair of a parents' group at my child's school. I do this because I feel this is one way in which I can intentionally live out my baptism in a self-conscious manner. It is my experience that intentional ministries work best when they have a beginning and an end—

even if we take them up again after we have had a break. Sometimes we need to say to people who are always doing something in the gathered church that they need a year in the scattered church for their sense of balance, or vice versa. Sometimes we might need to say to Joe who takes on every job in the church that no one else wants, 'Joe, maybe this year, your intentional ministry needs to be to your family. They need you too.' I have a suspicion we don't say things like this enough.

Structures of Support

It is a primary maxim of ministry that we should never call forth a ministry in the name of Christ until a structure for support is firmly in place. This support might be as simple as one Christian saying to another, 'Mary, I will remember you each day in my prayers that your ministry might be fruitful', or it might be as structured as a regular weekly meeting of a group of people who read the Bible together and pray for one another in the work they do. I belong to two such groups—each very different from the other—and one that I have been a part of for over ten years. When I have fallen on my face, it is through this group of fellow Christians—companions in faith, that I have been lifted up and sent on my way again.

It is the task of the gathered church (either on a local, diocesan and national level) both to help the scattered church discern what ministries are needed, in addition to ministries of presence, and to provide the support and the training for their ministries to be carried out. Davida Foy Crabtree, a United Church of Christ minister in Colchester, Connecticut, writes in her book, *The Empowering Church*, how a congregation restructured itself to give greater support to its ministry when scattered during the week. The leadership of the congregation was organized to give support and direction in eight specific areas—these being the only ongoing committees in the life of the congregation. These eight committees were concerned about the whole church both scattered and gathered, but they were trying to strike a greater balance. The eight ministries which they developed were:

Ministry in the Workplace
Ministry in the Home

Ministry in Church Life
Ministry in the Community
Ministry of Stewardship
Ministry of Mission and Witness
Ministry of Education
Ministry of Gifts and Leadership

Although the establishment of these areas took a lot of effort and required major changes in priority, it resulted in a whole new sense of what the church was about and the church in this small town began to grow. 'Every church needs a rhythm of movement between corporate ministry and individual ministry', Dee Crabtree writes, 'between nurturing members within their own spheres of need and drawing them out beyond themselves, between institutional renewal for the sake of the world and institutional abandonment for the sale of the world. This mission component is (always) the crucial next step'.[1]

What I find especially refreshing in the organizational model that this congregation offers, is the balance given to ministry within the gathered church and ministry in the scattered church throughout the community. Although we speak a lot about the importance of family life in the Christian community there is not much attention given to training men and women for the ministry of parenthood, and yet, when you stop to think about it, the ministry of a parent is the fundamental ministry by which Christian family life is sustained. A parish committee responsible for ministry in the home would make sure that new parents in the congregation were given help in what it means to be a parent, but would also be concerned with the quality of life in the surrounding community.

There are congregations now that have discernment groups that meet to discern where the ministry of the church is most needed and to discern what members of the congregation have the gifts needed to carry these ministries out, and then to call them forth with a system of support and evaluation in place. I suspect that most parishes still don't think in these terms, but when the call to mission is heard, renewal begins to happen The reason it happens is the church is not something we have created. The church is God's creation—that community of faith through which, by the power of the Spirit, the Risen Christ makes himself known to the world.

Training for Mission

In the past year two studies have been published for circulation within the Episcopal Church in the United States that deal directly with training for mission in the context of the Decade of Evangelism. The first document is the report of the Standing Commission on Evangelism prepared for the General Convention of the Episcopal Church which met in Phoenix, Arizona in July 1991.[2] The second study is entitled *Called to Mission*[3] and contains the finding of the Mission Discernment Project initiated in 1988 by the Executive Council of the Episcopal Church. The value of both of these documents lies in their fascinating description of those programmes that have been initiated where mission has become the acknowledged focus of congregational life.

The report of the Standing Committee on Evangelism[4] begins with a strong statement on the theology of evangelism and its implication for the Church's call to mission today. The evangelistic mission of the church seems to be strongest in those situations where priority is given to personal transformation with congregational life, where congregations themselves are concerned with their own renewal, where bishops and dioceses provide visionary leadership and where prayer for the conversion of the world is seen as critical to the church's life. 'We need to recognize', the report points out, 'that baptism is both a grace-filled encounter with the Lord and a moment that seeks (or awaits) a decision . . . The sad fact is that in the Episcopal Church many have been sacramentalized without ever being evangelized. We need to call for decision not only from those beyond the Church, but even from those within it'.[5]

Within this framework the report cites five elements that seem necessary for an effective mission strategy and then notes a number of quite different congregations where these elements are present. 'Our goal', states the report, 'is to encourage the kind of congregations in which evangelism is incorporated into the fabric of community life . . . No one strategy or method will be appropriate for every congregation across our varied Church. But some common elements emerge from the commission's experience during the past triennium'.

'First we have discovered that every congregation committed to evangelistic ministry is one in which the scriptures are believed seriously and taught systematically.

'Second, we have discovered that an evangelistic congregation needs a vision for its life and ministry. In other words, the congregation must discover what might be called its 'godly distinction'.

'Third, we have discovered that an evangelistic congregation needs to identify unevangelized persons or groups in its vicinity.

'Fourth, we have discovered that an evangelistic congregation needs to develop strategies consistent with its godly distinctives and with the needs of the persons being evangelized.

'Fifth, congregations need to look at themselves through the eyes of a newcomer. Is the liturgy understandable? Is worship alive in a way that draws people?'[6]

With these criteria in mind the report examines the mission strategies of eight congregations that are quite different in make-up, size and theological perspective. But clearly in each of these diverse congregations small group Bible study is firmly established, a clear sense of relationship to the surrounding community has been articulated and the congregation has articulated for itself a clear sense of identity—when it is that makes this particular congregation special.

The research study which culminated in the publication of *Called to Mission* is much broader in scope focusing on those many aspects by which a variety of congregations bring the message of the gospel to the world around them. St Philip's Church in San Jose, California (Diocese of El Camino Real) is a congregation composed of five separate distinct ethnic and cultural congregations within the larger parish, each with its own warden, services and leaders.[7] In a congregation of some five hundred members, 45 are Hispanic, 150 Laotian, 25 Afro-Americans, 175 Anglo-Americans, 100 Filipinos, and 15 from other groups including Native Americans, Indians and Pacific Islanders. St George's Church in Fredericksburg, Virginia is totally different but like St Philip's, was able to re-order its priorities and restructure the environment of congregational life to such a degree that the church was free to respond to the leading of the Spirit in ways that at first would not have seemed possible. The value of the case studies described in *Called to Mission* lies in the variety of situations which are presented. But, like the report from the Commission on Evangelism, there are a number of elements that all of these congregations have in common. In training the congregation for mission all, in one degree or another, seemed to have the following programmatic elements built into the life of the congregation and involving a significant number of people including those who were looked upon as leaders. These elements include:

1. A variety of small group experiences that enabled people to embrace the story of redemption in their own lives. These experiences ranged from diocesan sponsored programmes aimed at helping people live out the implication of their baptism to structured programmes of ongoing Bible study including the widely used Education for Ministry programme developed by the School of Theology of the University of the South.[8]

2. The development of a group within the life of the congregation whose ministry involved discerning the work of the Spirit in the larger community and calling forth the gifts of the membership to respond to the challenge that this presented. The identification of the primary mission to which a church is called in the light of the particular gifts a congregation has been given is critical to any effective mission strategy.

3. A well-developed system for ministries both within the gathered and scattered church. In the congregation that was studied, a lot of emphasis was given to the shared ministry of laity and clergy and the sense of equality that this implies as well as an emphasis aimed at bridging the gap between personal faith and everyday life. One of the most personally satisfying experiences I have ever had within the life of the church involved participation in a group of business and professional people concerned with ethical issues in their work and what it means to be a Christian ministering in the scattered church. What was important was not so much the resolving of ethical dilemmas but the discovery of a mutuality that we did not know we had. It is this sense of interconnectedness with others who share in the ministry of the gospel which is at the heart of life in Christ.

4. In every church that these studies described, prayer and worship were seen as central to the church's mission. In almost every case, a heightened sense of mission was directly related to a heightened sense of the importance of prayer and concern for the vitality of worship, including a well worked out system of hospitality by which new and lapsed members, as well as members who felt left out by the changes that occurred, were included into the Eucharistic fellowship and given a part to play.

Mission always involves ongoing programme and structured change. You cannot talk about responding to the call of the Spirit while at the same time worrying about how we are going to keep things the way they have always been. People's feelings and opinions are important as changes are made but you cannot be responsive to the gospel imperative without the willingness to let go long enough for the Spirit to lead the way. Having said this, however, it is also important to remind ourselves again that what makes a difference in the life of the church is not new structures, which, of course, may help, but that inner transformation of each baptized member that comes about as a result of a personal encounter with Jesus Christ. The renewal of the church is not primarily a matter of management but of emersion, a change of heart that opens us in trust to the movement of the Spirit in human life. The disciples did not go out into the world with the good news of Jesus Christ as the result of a committee assignment. They burst out upon the world because they had a story to tell and an experience to share. And what they were then, we are now—men and women with a story to tell and an experience to share—women and men baptized into Christ, gathered and scattered and marked as Christ's own forever. This is what mission is all about.

Notes

1. Davida Foy Crabtree, *The Empowering Church*, Alban Institute Publications, p. 58
2. Report of the Standing Commission on Evangelism to the 1991 General Convention of the Episcopal Church. Office of Evangelism, Episcopal Church Center, 815 Second Avenue, New York, NY 10017.
3. *Called to Mission*, John Docker, Ann Rowthorn and Wayne Schwab ed., Office of Ministry Development, 815 Second Avenue, New York, NY 10017.

4. Report of the Standing Commission on Evangelism, op cit., p. 108
5. ibid, p. 112. 113.
6. *Called to Mission*, op cit., p. 18
7. Two diocesan programs now in wide use throughout the US are 'Living our Baptismal Covenant' (Diocese of Milwaukee) and 'Living Into Our Baptism' developed by John Westerhoff and Caroline Hughes, Episcopal Church Center, 1987.
8. Education for Ministry (EFM), School of Theology, University of the South, Sewanee, Tennessee. See also The Catechumenal Process: Adult Initiation and Formation for Christian Life and Ministry, The Church Hymnal Corporation, 800 Second Avenue, New York, NY 10017. 1990.

9

RENEWAL OF THE CHURCH IN MISSION

The Work of the Spirit in Christian Formation

Sehon Goodridge

In a real sense the Church is faced with a situation of crisis and restlessness. In our pilgrimage of faith there comes the moment when God's presence breaks through in judgement, challenging our complacency, security and self-righteousness. This is a critical moment; a response has to be made. If the response is one of trustful obedience to God whose good purposes and promises are ever sure, we shall see a door of opportunities open for effectual witness to him in the world. Indeed we shall experience a restlessness which is not primarily a characteristic of the world, but the renewing and recreative presence of the Spirit summoning us to witness to the 'new creation', the 'new people of God', within the social and cultural changes of our time. While therefore the Church takes changes in society into account in its services, and in its forms of organisation and communication, it must not concentrate solely on an adaptation to changed social conditions.[1] It must concentrate on its inner renewal by the Spirit who judges as well as renews, and who never allows us to settle down, 'at ease in Sion'.

What is Renewal?

Our attention has been called to the different ways in which the word 'renewal' is understood and used:

> Indeed, the word 'renewal' is often used ambiguously. It can be used in different contexts to mean different things. For most writers renewal has a positive connotation, but they ask, 'What kind of renewal are you looking for?' One of the problems is that some are concerned with their 'identity' and the maintenance of the integrity

of the community; others want to make their witness credible in the prevailing circumstances. For the first, renewal appears as a threat because it may challenge their tradition by calling upon them to rethink their theological affirmations. The others fear that by not becoming credible, by not responding relevantly to a situation, they will be unfaithful to the Gospel.[2]

When we consider further that the word 'renewal' has been linked variously with evangelical and Charismatic movements, we see how inclusive a word 'renewal' has become. For our purposes we understand renewal as the process by which the local Church faces the challenge of crisis, responds in a new way to its vocation of forming disciples, and witnessing in the power of the Spirit to the graciousness of God and the Lordship of Christ.

Renewal begins in Crisis

The process of renewal begins in the challenge of crisis. There is the heightened awareness that faith has flagged, that vision is beclouded, that fellowship is anaemic, that the worship is uninspiring, and that witness is feeble, amidst the apathy and cynicism of our contemporary society. When we examine the structures of the Church we may well ask whether they facilitate, or inhibit, growth and witness. There is also the concern for a new vision and adequate resources. These stages of renewal have been well defined for us:

> The challenge of crisis begins the process. Whether spiritual renewal is personal or corporate, the ongoing experiences of everyday Christian Life or the landmark experience of the contemporary renewal movements, it goes through three identifiable stages. First of all comes *crisis*, a challenge (either external or internal) that brings us up short, which does not allow us to continue along our present path without response and adjustment. Secondly, a *search* for the right response, and for the resources to carry it out, an attempt to break through on a spiritual level. Thirdly, the *breakthrough itself*, bringing new insights, fresh resources, new purpose and direction . . .[3]

There is a clear recognition that there must be a *metanoia*, a change of direction, propelled by a confidence in God's renewing and enabling grace and power.

135

Personal and Communal Renewal

Discipleship is an integral part of the process of renewal. When the Gospel of Jesus Christ encounters a human being in the power of the Spirit, a new reality is created. This is an experience that takes us beyond ourselves to God himself, to the fullness of his life in Jesus Christ. Renewal may thus mean investing human existence with the grace of God as energy for life and light in the world. Where life and light combine there are no boundaries. Mission cannot therefore be separated from the spiritual formation and journey of discipleship. The mission of the Church cannot ignore those who are bearing the life and light of Christ.

The renewal of personal faith, life and witness is followed by a renewal of relationships, of community, of mission. The encounter with God's love evokes a response of love towards him, our fellow human beings and indeed towards the whole creation. As love flows out, spiritual vitality is maintained; relationships are healed; relational groups are sustained; the Body of Christ is discovered, and active concern for the poor and disabled is maintained.[4] Spiritual power is released by the offering and receiving of forgiveness. Loneliness is swallowed up in fellowship groups that are welcoming, caring and healing. Equality of status becomes the mark of the family of God; differences of race, culture and gender bear no hierarchical distinctions. Indeed we discover that the supreme mark of the leader is servanthood. We discover also that to be renewed by God's grace and mercy is to become aware of a new solidarity with those who suffer injustice, and experience various disabilities. With personal and communal renewal comes the experience of being a new community under the authority, and in the presence, of the risen and exalted Lord. Such a community rejects discrimination against persons or groups, and opens to genuine conversation, participation and service:

> This community draws its values from the crucified and risen Lord, who determines its spirituality. It manifests itself as a witnessing and eucharistic community (Acts 2. 41, 44). The Spirit gives its name *Koinonia* to the people of God, transforming it into a church for others, a community turning outwards from inside the ghetto, searching for the quality of human life, for new lifestyles and values.[5]

We must ask ourselves whether the Church is a place where people have a new experience of Christ (spiritual formation and growth), a new sense of community (transformed relationships) and a vision of a new creation (participation in God's recreative activity).

Public and Liberative Spirituality

The Spirit regenerates the people of God, constituting them as Church, and transforming and empowering them for mission. This participation in, and witness to, the Spirit interfaces with a 'success' and a 'consumerism' culture in which life is valued by our attainment of wealth and power, and by what we can buy, own, use and sell. The image of God, the reflection of the soul and spirit, can be perverted by symbols of immortality based on greed and power. The idolatry of wealth and power must therefore be unmasked. Herein lies the intrinsic relationship between spiritual formation and mission, as 'rebellious powers' which enslave, dehumanise, and divide human beings are named and dethroned. Indeed, 'we are not contending against flesh and blood, but against principalities, against powers, against the world rulers of this present darkness, against the spiritual host of wickedness in heavenly places'. Eph. 6.12.

Elsewhere I have argued for a prophetic, public and liberative spirituality which commits us to a struggle against idolatry and evil forces:

Christian, incarnational spirituality commits us, however, to a view of the total person in a total context. This is no over-emphasis on idealism or a flight of escapism. Rather, there is an engagement in relationships, transforming them from being oppressive and exploitative to being liberative and celebrative. Such are the characteristics of people's freedom movements across the globe in the post-World War Two period. This then is a spirituality in the struggle for human liberation based on justice, peace and love. It is an engaged spirituality and not one that is merely private, idealistic and intellectual.[6]

137

Jesus himself has shared his consciousness of the integral relationship between spiritual formation and public, liberative mission:

> The Spirit of the Lord is upon me,
> because he has anointed me to preach good news to the poor.
> He has sent me to proclaim release to the captives
> and recovering of sight to the blind,
> to set at liberty those who are oppressed,
> to proclaim the acceptable year of the Lord.
>
> Luke 4.18-19

Such a spirituality points to a holistic view, a vision of a world turned upside down, to include the deepest aspirations and longings of those who are on the underside of this world.

The Spirit and Empowerment

God's forgiveness through Christ is sheer gift, and when human beings accept it, the way is open for a new life of empowerment. The gift of the Spirit in baptism signals a break from destructive self-centredness to a living fellowship, not of like-minded persons in an association, but of believers who have all things in common and who are intent on bearing urgent witness to their faith. When Christian disciples realise their status as sons and daughters of God, they also assume the responsibility of living this new life in the world. Gal. 4.4ff; 5.25.

The nature of Power for Christians is discovered 'in identification with Christ's way of self-emptying, self-sacrifice, suffering in solidarity with all victims of human hurt or natural affliction, and self-oblation to the will of the Father.'[7] The Church as a whole, in its structures and ministry, must exercise power in accordance with the model of Christ's self-emptying and sacrificial love, giving voice to the voiceless, hope to the hopeless, and power to the powerless. In the life of the Spirit personal and corporate power will be marked by self-giving and service and not by self-seeking and dominance. No organisation, including the Church, can exist without some form of structure and patterns of authority. But the Church must uphold a model of power that challenges the worldly model of dominance. The following guidelines have been sketched for us:

First, both the attitude with which we approach our life in an institutional Church, and also the way in which we answer ingrained patterns of social interaction, can be affected by the power in the Spirit which we have been discussing, and they must be held open to it.

Second, this power in the Spirit will be reflected in the quality of the institutional Church's common life, particularly as it is expressed in the activity of prayer and worship. Here it is that the Church, ever aware of its own weakness and imperfection, is (or should be) particularly open to receiving the power of the Spirit.

Third, the Church, the Church's authority and structures are never ends in themselves, but exist only for the service of God and in dependence on God. Given a firm grasp of this truth, the Church should actually feel itself relieved that it is of little worldly consequence, indeed should delight in and perhaps boast of that fact, that the power of Christ may rest upon it.[8]

Many Christians have lost sight of the fact that they are Christ's servants in the world, and that the Church becomes the Church in serving the world. An essential aspect of the renewal of the Church is a focus on this vocation to be the Church in the world.

Renewal movements and ministries have challenged the Church with a commitment to prayer and praise, and a rediscovery of an unimpeded participation in the Spirit, which draws us into union with Christ. Proper emphasis has been placed on the gifts of the Spirit for prophetic-type ministries and miraculous powers. It is the Spirit who empowers all the gifts and distributes them to each one as he wills. The spirit endows individuals with gifts, not to serve their own personal interests or to foster a sense of superiority, but 'for the common good', for building up the Christian community for effective witness in the world. The Spirit empowers and equips the Church, not for its own sake, but for its ministry and mission. (1 Cor. 12.12-27; Eph. 4.1-16).

The Spirit and Christian Leadership

In the Spirit-filled community, members have their respective gifts and functions. All are called to ministry and mission; there is no distinction between active and passive members, between those who give and those who receive. Elsewhere I have called attention to the work of the Spirit in maintaining the inner connection between inclusive ministry and total witness:

> The Christian ministry of witness, service and reconciliation is not just one task among others; it is an essential work of the Church. This ministry has its origin in God himself who has acted in history on behalf of people all down the ages, and has raised up men and women to interpret his acts of creating and sustaining, redeeming, judging, healing and reconciling. Above all, the very nature and purposes of God were uniquely and decisively disclosed in the person, ministry, death and resurrection of Jesus Christ. When we have discovered this givenness of the ministry in Jesus Christ, sustained by the presence and power of the Holy Spirit, we can understand our place in this ministry by virtue of our baptism. We can understand also the way in which the Holy Spirit enables us to use our gifts in the Body of Christ—such gifts as knowledge, wisdom, administration, healing, faith, prayer and service. With this variety of gifts will go a variety of functions within the total ministry of the Church. These include witness in family life and daily work, responsible participation in secular organisations and professions, and in the ordained ministry as a special function within the one ministry of the Church. It is with this perspective that we approach the questions of Christian leadership.[9]

If the Spirit forms and enables all for leadership, then the distinction between the 'teaching Church' (the clergy) and the 'learning Church' (the laity) must disappear. Also relationships of domination and dependence between clergy and laity must not be fostered.

The task of forming Christian leadership is largely a theological one. In theological education there is the continuous tension between the logos and the Spirit, between the rationality of critical study and the transcendence of the object of that study which is God. Theological discourse and the scientific study of the Bible tend to exclude the spiritual dimension. This latter is reserved for devotion, meditation and worship. This dichotomy between the rational and the spiritual must not be allowed in the formation of Christian leadership. In the process of formation theological discourse and the critical study of the Bible can come alive as sources of spirituality:

> The other 'key' of critical study is the analysis of *reality*. It is not possible to begin with an abstraction of God in relation to the human reality: God is present there as an active presence, as a prerequisite for change or revolution, as he who announces judgement, as power (this is what the word 'Spirit/spiritual' means) for transformation. The God who *mobilizes* the human being lets himself be seen in critical study insofar as it completes the closed circuit with reality. God is not present in books but in life. For this reason, critical study (with its consciousness-raising and analytical contribution) based in the concrete life of the surrounding human community, reverberates spiritually in the one who learns theology and Bible.[10]

With this perspective of theological education in Christian formation for leadership, 'theology' is not the preserve of the academic and the clerical, but is open to all disciples, male and female, in various cultural contexts. One envisages a group of clergy and laity engaged in theological exploration seeking the Spirit's illumination and empowerment for action. There have been testimonies from numerous persons who have experienced renewal, growth and potential for leadership through the media of 'house groups' and 'base communities'. They have learnt to see, to judge and to act. They have experienced the glorious liberty of the children of God; they have experienced the freedom and spontaneity of witness and proclamation. What also emerges is a new pattern of spirituality, a lay spirituality, suited to their needs and witness in the world.

In a real sense the task before the Church in its renewal for mission is the formation of spiritual leadership. When we use the word 'spiritual' we are asserting the vital reality of human existence. We are not affirming the duality of body and spirit; we are not emphasising that matter is here and spirit is elsewhere in some form of other-worldly existence. We are asserting that body and spirit, matter and spirit are inextricably bound together. Body must be viewed in relation to spirit, and matter in relation to spirit. For this reason William Temple, drawing on the

141

principle of the incarnation, could affirm that Christianity is the most materialistic of all religions. In similar vein I have shared the following insights:

> ... It is in this view of the world and of a nation, both of their material and spiritual elements, that there will be hope of making human both politics and economics. It is in this same view of persons that will lie the future of the human race, and will serve to check all tendencies, agencies and incarnate 'principalities and powers' which reduce men and women to matter devoid of spirit. Christian leadership must stand against any forces that propagate a reductionist view of man, that he is only to be fed, watered and sheltered, while his very humanum, his worth, his freedom, in short, his spirit—all that is distinctively 'I'—is destroyed. The spirit of our Caribbean peoples has been deeply wounded and brutally battered in the past precisely because of the reductionist view of man. The exercise of spiritual leadership is nothing else than helping our fellowmen grow to maturity and self-fulfilment in truly humanizing and liberating structures and relationships.[11]

The Spirit announces new possibilities and summons clergy and laity alike, the *laos* (people) of God, Christian men and women, to shared ministry in the structures of the Church and in the structures of the world.

Conclusion

The missionary *motif* and the missionary enterprise have been significantly modified, in recognition that the Church is not only the recipient of God's grace, but also of his judgement. Judgement indeed has begun in 'the household of God'. The clarion call for repentance has been sounded. With repentance there is also the experience of renewal and the Spirit announces new possibilities. The people of God are in a time of paradigm change, a time of crisis where danger and opportunity meet. It is the Spirit that enables us to hold the creative tension between the old and the new, and sets the agenda for personal and communal renewal. It is the Spirit that regenerates, liberates and empowers for total ministry and mission.

When we are hemmed in by various strictures and structures the Spirit modifies and re-orientates our lives that we may have new horizons and new paths. We have a new awareness of the Spirit who stimulates and strengthens us, who makes us grow to maturity and emboldens us to witness. When this is experienced in the local Church, the Church-in-mission is realised. There is a clear need for Christian formation which will enable the people of God to witness to their faith in all spheres of life, and in the context of a scientific and technocratic society.

We must be reminded that mission is not primarily an activity of the Church, but an attribute of God. God is a missionary God:

> It is not the Church that has a mission of salvation to fulfil in the world; it is the mission of the Son and the Spirit through the Father that includes the church, creating a church as it goes on its way. It is not the church that administers the Spirit as the Spirit of preaching, the Spirit of the sacraments, the Spirit of the ministry or the Spirit of the tradition. The Spirit 'administers' the church with the events of word and faith, sacrament and grace, offices and traditions. If the church understands itself, with all its tasks and powers, in the Spirit and against the horizon of the Spirit's history, then it also understands its particularity as one element in the power of the Spirit and has no need to maintain its special power and its special charges with absolute and self-destructive claims.[12]

We do well to recall the missionary paradigm in the Lukan writings (Luke-Acts) in which the Spirit not only initiates and guides mission, but also empowers for mission. This is evident in the boldness of the witnesses once they have been endowed with the Spirit.

Notes

1. Jürgen Moltmann, *The Church in the Power of the Spirit*, SCM 1977, p. 3.
2. Ion Bria, ed., *People Hunger to be Near God*, Geneva, WCC/RCL, 1990, p. 29.
3. Josephine Bax, *The Good Wine: Spiritual Renewal in the Church of England*, Church House Publishing, London, 1986, p. 21.
4. Graeme Murray, 'Renewal of the Local Congregation For Mission' in *International Review of Mission* Vol. LXXX No.317, January 1991, p. 51. See also *Many Gifts, One Spirit*, report of ACC7, Singapore 1987, Church House Publishing, p. 34.
5. Ion Bria, 'Renewal in Mission: Challenge and Response' in *International Review of Mission*, ibid p. 57.

6. Sehon Goodridge, 'Spirituality and Justice' in *Spirituality and Mission, Report of the Proceedings of The Board of Mission Council, Church in Wales,* February 1991, p. 29.

7. *We Believe in the Holy Spirit*, The Doctrine Commission of the Church of England, Church House Publishing, 1991, p. 102.

8. Ibid., pp. 110-111.

9. Sehon Goodridge, 'Christian Leadership in the Caribbean' in *Moving Into Freedom*, K. Davis (ed.), Cedar Press, Barbados, 1977, pp. 3-4.

10. Samuel Amirtham and Robin Pryor (eds.) *Resources for Spiritual Formation in Theological Education*, WCC, PTE, Geneva, 1991 pp. 14-15.

11. Sehon Goodridge, 'Christian Leadership in the Caribbean', op. cit., p. 7.

12. Jürgen Moltmann, op. cit., pp. 64-65.

10

STRUCTURES AND STRATEGIES FOR MISSION AND EVANGELISM—SABAH STYLE

Yong Ping Chung

I. Introduction

The general disquiet and dissatisfaction within the Anglican Communion on the structure and strategy of our Church in Mission and Evangelism is clearly highlighted by the MISAG I Report:

> Though there are notable exceptions, the dominant model of the Church within the Anglican Communion is a pastoral one. Emphasis in all aspects of Church's life tends to be placed on care and nurture rather than proclamation and service.[1]

When the Bishops of the Anglican Communion 'brought their Dioceses to Lambeth' in 1988, the same disquiet and dissatisfaction was reflected and a response was attempted. The call to a Decade of Evangelism pin-pointed evangelism as the key to a new strategy for mission. Resolution 44 called for a shift of strategy from the traditional model of care and nurture to 'a dynamic missionary' model of 'proclamation and service'. Each local diocese and church was also challenged to re-examine its 'Church structure, patterns of worship and ministry' and to look to God for a new strategy through 'the fresh movement of the Holy Spirit.'[2] This, to borrow the words of the Anglican Consultative Council Meeting (ACC 6), Badagry, Nigeria 1984, is an 'enormous work of reconstruction and reform.'[3]

Faced with such an enormous and complicated subject, I begin to feel like the blind men in the Hindu story entitled 'The Blind Men and the Elephant'.

The Blind Men and the Elephant

Three blind men sit around an elephant and argue about what an elephant is like. The first blind man, touching the tail of the elephant, says 'An elephant is like a snake' The second blind man, stroking the leg of the elephant, says, 'An elephant is like the trunk of a tree.' The third blind man, feeling the flank of the elephant, says 'An elephant is like a wall.'

No matter which part of the elephant each of the blind men touched, it is only a tiny part of the elephant. Similarly, whatever I write in the following pages, is at best only a little tiny portion of the huge and complicated subject. The choice is either to shout 'an elephant is like . . .' or to keep silence. I chose to accept the assignment of writing this chapter because I hope by so doing I can share our Sabah stories as well as enticing and encouraging more blind men to share their version of the elephant. Hopefully in time to come, by sharing our stories, we can all share in this 'enormous work of reconstruction and reform' and help our Churches to be effective in 'making Christ known in his world.' Here is the story from Sabah.

II. Context and History

The Diocese of Sabah is set in the context of a multi-racial, multi-religious, multi-cultural, multi-language society. Islam is the national religion. The 38,000 Anglicans spread out over an area of 76,392 sq. km. are a very tiny proportion (3 per cent) of the 1.3 million total population of the State of Sabah in the Eastern part of Malaysia. However, among the Christian denominations working in Sabah, we are the second largest body after the Roman Catholics.

In terms of history, we were the offshoot of the Missionary Movement in the nineteenth century. The first SPG (Society for the Propagation of the Gospel) missionary arrived in Sabah in 1888. We were first a part of the Diocese of Borneo. Most of our early Churches were established on the coastal towns of the then British North Borneo among the Chinese. In the early 1950s, effort was made to reach out to the Kadazan/Dusun people in the Interior of Sabah. As a result of the steady growth of this interior work, we were carved out of the Diocese of Borneo and formed into a new Diocese of Sabah in July 1962.

Needless to say, the new Diocese so formed was patterned after the well-known structure of the Anglican model with its

Archdeaconries, Parishes, Churches and Mission Districts and it was ministered to by Bishop, Priests and Deacons. While we record with deep gratitude the zeal, dedication and sacrifices of our missionary forerunners in bringing and sharing the Gospel with our people in Sabah, we must also at the same time point out that with only a few exceptions, most of these missionaries, either by force of circumstances or by personal choice, did not stay in Sabah long enough really to establish long-term strategy and effect structural change in the Diocese for mission and evangelism. Yet it was in such a familiar Anglican structure of a Diocese that God taught and continues to teach us the need to adapt our structure for effective carrying out of our strategy for mission and evangelism in our context.

III. Two Pictures

As we look back to our history, at the time of the formation of our Diocese, we can see two pictures.

In the town areas, the churches were dominated by clergy. Many of them were wonderful pastors. They singlehandedly, with great vigour and outstanding courage, carried the burden of the ministries of the Church. They cared for and pastored those already in the Church with real distinction. But little concerted effort was put into outreach and evangelism as we know it today. Converts were mainly won through the young people in the schools. These as a matter of fact were far and few between. Church records show that child baptism by far outnumbered adult baptism.

On the other hand, the picture in the interior of Sabah was very different. In the Interior Mission, as we began the work, we had only one priest, an Iban from Sarawak, one nurse and one school teacher, also an Iban. They arrived to start the mission from scratch, so to speak. They built the church, clinic and school. But most important of all, they shared their faith with the people. New converts were won by the hundreds. Adult baptism was the norm in the new and young church. Despite the shortage of workers and money, the work that started on one river soon was quickly spread to other rivers. Today, we work on five rivers.

147

IV. Our First Lesson

This over-simplified review and analysis of the two situations helps us to learn our first important lesson about structure and strategy in mission and evangelism. The town churches did not make many converts because they were enslaved by their pastoral structure in mentality and reality. So much effort and energy of the priest were absorbed in caring and nurturing for the church people. Very little was left to make any strategy for evangelism. But in the Interior Mission this was different. The strategy was clear. The workers were sent to make converts. There was little cumbersome structure to burden the task of evangelism. In fact the whole reason for the existence of the Interior Mission was to promulgate the Gospel and win souls for Christ. Thus we learned the danger of enslaving structure. Thus we learned the importance of a clear goal and strategy for mission and evangelism.

V. The Wind of Change

These two pictures of the town Churches and Interior Churches persisted for a while. We were neither ready nor able and willing to change. Meanwhile God was changing the landscape of our country. The Government began to require the Church to be Malaysianised. A persecution broke out in Sabah. In a matter of two to three years, all expatriate workers were asked to leave. The Anglican Church in Sabah that had for many years depended on Western missionary staff to pastor its people was caught unprepared. It was in this kind of turmoil God's Holy Spirit blew all over Sabah. General revival took place in all churches. The wind of change, the hard time, was used by the good Lord to teach us further about strategy and structure. With just a handful of local clergy left to man a huge Church (in land areas at least), we were desperate. We were driven to our knees. Overnight, many structures would have to be changed. The parish system of one priest for one church, known so well to us, could no more be maintained. There were not enough priests to go round the Diocese and pastor the people. The normal way of training a priest took at least four years. Time was not on our side. To maintain sacramental life, we needed to break new ground. Within a short period of three to four years, five senior laymen with little formal theological training were ordained non-stipendiary priests. This was indeed a very refreshing and bold break-through. Up to today we still reap the benefits of this new venture. We intend to continue to challenge our older men to answer the call to be ordained non-stipendiary priests. To maintain the over-all ministries of the Church, we need to depart from our previous clergy dominating and clergy centred structure.

Lay training—to train the lay people to take a full and active part in the ministries of the Church—was started everywhere. On our knees and out of necessity, the good Lord forced us into taking the biblical concept of the priesthood of all believers and partner-ship of laity and clergy seriously. As a result, the shape and structure of our ministry team begin to change. We began to sense that the traditional threefold ministry of Bishop, Priest and Deacon that has served us well is not sufficient to cope with the ministry of the Church, if the Church is to take its mission and evangelism seriously. We began to realise that to confine the whole ministerial team only to the traditional threefold ministries is undoubtedly keeping the ministry of God in captivity. By doing so we fell into the trap of the strategy of the devil to slow down the work of the Church. To counter the enemy's strategy, we needed to release the ministry into the hands of the people of God. Thus we began the concept and strategy of widening the base for ministries. This meant we needed to create more categories of workers beside the traditional threefold ministries in the Church. This immediately transformed our structure for ministries.

Today we are organised into two Archdeaconries with seven self-supporting churches, ten non-self-supporting churches and seven Mission Districts which have a total of 70 big and small churches. To look after these churches and to carry on our mission and evangelism effectively, we have created many more categories of workers. In our Diocese at the moment, we have one Bishop, fourteen priests (two of these are also Archdeacons), four non-stipendiary priests, ten parish workers (male and female), three evangelists and fifteen youth evangelists. Even these are by no means a sufficient number of workers to do our work effectively. We thank God that we can count on a host of our lay people, after training, to participate in the many vital ministries of the Church. Lay persons leading worship; Bible study groups; prayer groups; lay people teaching baptism and confirmation classes, following up new believers, counselling, witnessing, etc. are common happenings each day in our Diocese now. All these have a deep impact on the whole structure and strategy of our Church. Today in the diocesan level, as well as the parish and mission district levels, our lay people in partnership with our clergy and lay workers take an equal part in making all decisions, spiritual and material, for the Church. What was started as a response to necessity for survival, has now become a useful and important step God has taken to change our structure and strategy for our mission and evangelism in Sabah.

VI. Our Responses

However, if we are honest at all, we have to admit that we were in fact very slow to respond to the challenge of our time. As an Anglican Diocese, we were by nature very cautious, by structure top-heavy, and had no strategy. Yet in our slow way, we identified our problems, we carefully conducted seminars, organised consultations and made experiments. Step by step we arrived at what we are today. This is by no means a simple and easy process. There are many factors and interplay of cause and effect that are still used by God to change us. The following are some of the major causes that shaped us up to this point in our structure and strategy for mission and evangelism.

1. *The Born Again Experience*

When we became a diocese in 1962, most of our lay people were used to being looked after and pastored by priests. In any given church, if there was no priest, there would be little or no activities. Many of our Anglicans were faithful and dedicated Church members but a large proportion of our people did not really have the born-again experience. If I may be bold to say, at that time, even some of our clergy were like that. As a result, we had many nominal Church members. This is reflected in the large number of Christmas Communicants as compared to normal Sunday Communicants. Even today we still believe that more than 40 per cent of Anglicans in our Diocese are nominal Church members. Our first strategy was to preach, teach and talk about the biblical truth of new life in Jesus. Clergy and lay people alike were challenged to ask themselves the very fundamental question—do I know the Lord Jesus as my personal saviour? Have I repented of my sins? Have I invited Jesus to come into my life? The Bible talks about it. Jesus challenged the people to have a personal life in him. The Apostles' writings urge us to have a new life in Jesus. Why then should we not do so as this is taught us by our Lord, shown us by the early apostles and authorised by the Scriptures?

So with no apology, sermons were focused on this subject on Sundays. Special evangelistic missions were organised. Speakers from other denominations who know about this important subject well, were invited to come and conduct large missions and seminars. At the beginning, it was hard to convince our Church people that this was important and necessary. Many people, including some clergy, were offended. But the long-term impact of these works was the gathering by the Holy Spirit of groups of 'converted souls' throughout the Diocese who in turn, valued the conversion and new life in Jesus very much and who were willing to share that experience with others. Indeed, no strategy and structure can be really effective to carry out Christ's mission and evangelism if the Church does not have the people who know the Lord Jesus personally, who listen and obey him faithfully; who out of their own life experience can share Jesus with their fellow-men. Mission and evangelism are involved in spiritual life-imparting work. Only those who have this life in Jesus are able to share that life with others.

This realisation also gave rise to the policy in the Diocese that every candidate accepted for full-time and ordination training must first be able to testify that he/she has a personal relationship with the Lord Jesus. The congregations were also taught to elect spiritually alive men and women onto Parish Church Councils and other leadership positions in the Church. All this may sound very unAnglican. But we praise God that it is biblical. Thus we learn that the most important strategy of the Church in mission and evangelism is to take the fundamental truth declared by Jesus himself, 'You must be born again', in spirit and in truth. Without changed life in the Church, there can never be structure and strategy that can change life for the Church. Mission and evangelism are about changing lives for Jesus.

151

2. *The Development of Personal Bible Study: Daily Devotional Life and Bible Study Groups/Prayer Groups/Home Cell Groups*

Like other traditional Anglican Dioceses, for many years in our Diocese church attendance and receiving Holy Communion on Sundays, were considered as sufficient for one to be called a good Christian. Personal Bible study was nominally urged but never strongly pursued. Personal daily devotion was practically unheard of. Thus we discovered that most of our Church members were very superficial Christians. At best, they were good churchgoers, at worst many involved themselves in occult and other superstitious practices. Many were very nominal Christians who knew very little about Christ and the Christian faith. We realised that our system of one sermon—some were very short sermons indeed—a week would never be sufficient to sustain the spiritual growth of our people. Thus a very strong effort was put in to encourage and help our people to develop the habit of personal Bible study and personal daily devotion. To help strengthen this habit to be absorbed in the Word of God various small Bible study groups were established. These groups are known in different places by different names, i.e. Bible Study Groups, Prayer Groups, Home Cell Groups. Whatever the name may be, the strategy was very clear—to help our members to learn to love the Word of God.

We began to train leaders so that these groups could all be led by lay leaders. Our ultimate goal and strategy was to involve every church-going member in a Bible Study Group. We are far from reaching this goal yet. But we see increasing numbers of our people are attracted to such groups. The impact of this strategy is already very apparent. As more people in our Diocese go into the scriptures and Christian fellowship, their own faith becomes stronger. As their faith grows, their conviction, out of their own study of the Word of God, to reach out in mission and evangelism is also growing. Thus each small Bible study group became not only a nurture group but also an outreach group. The group begins to pray and care for friends and to bring friends into the group and eventually lead these friends to Christ. Many of our new converts in the last few years were won this way. This is reflected by the increase of adult baptism in all our Churches. The excitement and encouragement to the group when a new convert is won can never be measured. This group also becomes the training ground for outreach and evangelism.

3. *Lay Training in the Diocese*

This was started as our response to the shortage of full-time workers during the early seventies. The policy in the Diocese was to allow each Parish/Church/Mission District to do its own training according to its own need. The Diocese would assist by inviting and paying for the cost of the trainer or materials needed for the training. Lay training became our top priority in our regional Partnership in Mission submission. For a while, there were as many lay training programmes as there were Churches in our Diocese. This had the advantage of using and training our laity at their own level, and also raised the consciousness of their part and share in the life of the Church. Later the Diocese joined together with the Diocese of Singapore to go into lay training more systematically. Manuals were written for the various stages of the training programmes. In fact, lay training and motivation of the laity of the Church to develop skills to take an active part in the ministry of the Church is one of the most significant strategies which shape our structure for effective mission and evangelism. This leads to my next point.

4. *Changing Pattern of Training Workers*

Various factors were at work in changing our pattern of training our workers.

(a) As our churches in the Diocese began to grow as a result of stepping up in the strategy of evangelism, we realized that we needed more trained workers. So we prayed and encouraged more of our people to offer themselves for training to the priesthood. But also as the result of lay training and the widening of the base for ministries, we also discovered that some of our young people were keen to be trained for ministries but they did not necessarily feel called to be ordained. This led to our departure from the normal Anglican practice of accepting and sponsoring only ordination candidates to be trained in theological colleges. We adopted a new strategy. Together with those for normal ordination we also sent our young men or women to theological colleges with the aim of training them, and for them to return to be full-time lay workers in our Churches. Indeed, we have benefited by the effective ministries of our full-time lay workers in the total structure of our ministerial team.

(b) The vast, scattered and fast growing areas of our Interior Mission in the rural areas demanded more workers than we could afford and produce in the traditional way. To meet the manpower need of these vast areas and to maintain the momentum of our evangelistic effort, we needed to be innovative. So we began the Youth Evangelist Programme in Bahasa Malaysia. The programme works in this way. Young people who finish high school are challenged to attend a two-week special training course on evangelism. During the training, they are taught only some very basic and limited skills. After that short training, two by two they are sent out to the villages for three months. They are expected to go from village to village and use what they have learnt repeatedly. After this initial three months of work, those who would like to continue as youth evangelists will be given another ten days of special training and then sent out for another three-six months. At the end of that period, they will be gathered again for more training before they are sent out. After they have worked as youth evangelists for two years, they will then be selected to go to Theological College for further training either to be priests or full-time lay workers.

This strategy has worked well for us. We have thus raised up a number of full-time workers, ordained and lay, who know what mission and evangelism really mean, because they have grown out of such an environment.

(c) As we studied the age structure of Malaysian population, we realised that 55 per cent of our population are 24 years old and under. As we researched into the population trend of the towns in Sabah, we saw the need of the great number of Chinese youths. This presents us with the urgency to evangelise the Chinese youth. Thus a similar programme of Youth Evangelist training was started in Chinese to reach out to the Chinese youths who dwell mostly in the urban town centres. It is our hope eventually to establish schools of evangelism in Chinese, English and Bahasa Malaysia to produce effective young evangelists whose sole function in the Church is to reach out and evangelise the young people in our State. This may be seen as a departure from our normal Anglican structure.

(d) *The Grass-roots Ministries.* As a Diocese we have, since our formation, worked mainly through our Mission Schools in the town areas. Hence, our town Churches are much more a middle class Church. But as we look at our population composition, we realise that the majority of our people are in the lower income group, normally classified as blue collar workers or grass-roots people. We need to make conscious efforts to reach out to them too, because this is what the great Commission demands of us. We praise God that through our youth work, some new converts were won from this group of people. When some of these new converts, without many formal academic qualifications, responded to the call of God to offer themselves to be trained for full-time work, we had a hard decision to make. They just did not fit into the traditional mode of training. The normal theological colleges would not accept them. But God in his own gracious way opened up doors for us. A Theological College in Singapore recognised the need and started a new department especially for the training of workers to work among the grass-roots people. We have five such students in training at the moment. In 1992 we look forward to the return of the first graduate from this school to help us to change our ministerial structure further as we set our strategy to reach out and evangelise among the grass-root people in Sabah.

The above description is in a way an over-simplification of some of the issues and measures that impinged upon our structure and strategy under the heading of *Changing Pattern of Training Workers.* Within a short space of less than ten years, as our Diocese became more and more aware of our fundamental task required of the Lord, we were presented with different challenges which demanded discernment and response. Without other experience to go by, we learned by trial and error. Now we can look back and praise God that all our responses were

155

guided by a clear vision—God required that the Church should go and evangelise—and a firm strategy—to go and share the Gospel so that souls may be won to Christ. We were willing to modify and change our structures and pattern of ministry in order to meet the challenges placed before us.

5. *The 'One Brings One' Strategy*

This was started in order to involve the whole people of God, young and old, in the task of evangelism. This is how it works. It is a voluntary programme promoted in the Churches. The person who had decided to join this programme was given a pledge card with a short prayer printed in it. This person pledged to pray for the salvation of one or two friends or relatives every day. After praying for a few months, he/she will then pray that God will give him/her the opportunity to witness/share the Gospel with these friends or relatives. This programme put into sharp focus the concept that each born again Christian has the obligation to share the Gospel. It also gives every willing member an opportunity to share the Gospel quietly with the person(s) known to and loved by him/her.

6. *Changing Pattern of Worship*

As people of different races, languages, ages, social status, education backgrounds are won to Christ, their needs, styles and tastes for worship are bound to be different. As an Anglican Diocese, we also have our own printed liturgy. But we find that we need to respond to the challenge and demand that will meet the spiritual need of our people in worship. The best solution we found is for the Diocese to have some minimum essentials in our diocesan liturgy which everyone needs to adhere to for unity and identity. Then each worker or priest is encouraged to explore with the congregation meaningful ways to express their sense of worship. The stereotype celebration of the Eucharist by the clergy alone during service is now replaced by services with full participation of the whole congregation. Services of lively congregational singing, clapping of hands, body language, lay people reading lessons, taking the intercessions, distributing the elements with the priest are now common practice in the Diocese. Many variations are permitted as the people of God come together in celebration and worship. We find that this changing pattern of worship strengthens the sense of community in every Church. Very often non-Christians find it easier to understand what Christian worship is all about when they see spontaneous responses.

7. *Prayer and Fasting*

The most powerful weapons, apart from the Scripture, God has given to his Church to do spiritual battle, are the disciplines of prayer and fasting. As revival touches the life of our people and we begin to awake to the fact that the spiritual battle we engage in is not against flesh and blood but against all principalities and the dark forces of the heavenly realm, we begin to take prayer and fasting very seriously. Many individuals in our Churches began to pray and fast for various matters. Many Churches also began to organise all day prayer and fasting for the whole Church. We witness the cumulating effect of such spiritual maturity and power. In many of our Churches we began to penetrate into the hard core believers of idol worshippers and Chinese folk religions. Many pagan altars are surrendered to be burnt when the owner comes to life in Jesus. The dark forces of the spirits can only be broken by spiritual power generated through prayer and fasting. Today our people can talk naturally about such experience and participate in such exercise. This experience helps us to realise that no matter how we adapt our structure and how we define our strategy, we need to have a strategy to motivate our people to pray and to fast. Man-made structures and strategy need to be owned by God. Prayer and fasting help us to discern the Lord's will and obey his desire and obediently hand over structure and strategy for his mission and to win souls for him.

VII. Influences of other Churches and Church Growth Seminars

Ministering in a multi-religious and minority situation, we cannot work in isolation. Co-operation with other denominations is imperative for good Christian witness and survival. Mission and evangelism and dealing with the Government are areas of ecumenical co-operation that can come very naturally in our situation. Churches often come together to plan city-wide and State-wide mission activities such as evangelistic crusades, mission nights, etc. This close co-operation has the effect of helping each denomination to be exposed to each other, their aspirations, structure, strategy and many other aspects of their Church life. We have very much benefited from this relationship because we learn much of our strategy and zeal from other outgoing Churches. The most important impact of this close relationship was the gathering of all the major denominations in Sabah for a Church Growth Seminar in 1988. During the Seminar, we worked out a common strategy for mission and evangelism. In this context of the extension of God's Kingdom in Sabah, each denomination also worked out its own target and strategy. We were very much encouraged and motivated by this Seminar. In June 1990 we followed up the Inter-Church Church Growth Seminar with our own Church Growth Seminar. Our strategy and the need for further changes to our structure is expressed in our final Statement adopted at the end of the Seminar.

VIII. Clear Vision of the World-wide Mission of the Church

As we worked on our strategy and adapted our structure, we reminded ourselves again and again that 'A Church that lives for itself will die by itself.' We are therefore very aware that we belong to a world-wide family—the Anglican Communion. Our mission in Sabah needs to be put into the context of the mission of the Church in our region and the world-wide Church. As a small and young Diocese, our contributions in terms of finances and human resources to the world-wide Church are very minimal. Yet we believe strongly that we can take an active part in the activities of our big family. We welcome every opportunity that allows our priests and workers to serve in the world-wide body. For example, my own participation in the Council of the Churches of East Asia, the Anglican Consultative Council,[4] USPG and other Partners in Mission Consultations was taken by our Diocese as part and parcel of our contribution and partnership to the mission of the world-wide Church. A clear vision of the world-wide mission of the Church is vital and important to sustain our own effectiveness in local mission and evangelism.

IX. Conclusion—The Movement of the Holy Spirit

'An elephant is like ...' Which part of the elephant have I described? One blind man can only describe one part of the elephant. The Sabah story is one of the multitudes of stories of how God, through the movement of his Holy Spirit, is changing the structures of the Churches in our Communion. As the Spirit of God touches the life of men and women he empowers them to minister to the world God so loves. He also puts into their hearts the burden for the salvation of all mankind through the proclamation of the Lord Jesus and the invitation of the lost souls to receive the new life in Jesus. When we respond obediently to this call, we fall into line with his strategy. This divine strategy will in turn mould, modify and change our structures so that we can be effective in our mission and evangelism for his glory.

If I be lifted up, I will draw all men unto me.

Notes

1. *Giving Mission its Proper Place*, Report of the first Mission Issues and Strategy Advisory Group, ACC, 1984, p. 5.
2. *The Truth Shall Make You Free*, The Lambeth Conference Report 1988, ACC, p. 231.
3. *Bonds of Affection*, Report of Proceedings of ACC-6, Badagry, Nigeria, 1984, ACC, p. 46.
4. Bishop Yong Ping Chung served on the ACC and was its Chairman 1984-90.

11

MISSION AND COMMUNICATION:
'ROGER AND OUT'

Roger Herft

Screens flash out the Great Commission

In the world of communication 'Roger and out' is a common but vital phrase. It tells you that 'your message has been received, understood and is being acted upon'. Glossy programmes, mission kit sets, multi-million dollar networks, fancy methods, slick gimmicks, have become a part of mission strategy as we enter the Decade of Evangelism. Public relations firms and advertising consultants seem to have entered the arena with zeal. Mission has become a high technology battle. David S. Barnett in his *Statistical Table on Global Mission* speaks of this megatrend. 'Since 1980 the Christian world has purchased and is using some 45 million computers with a capital value of no less than US$295 billion. These systems are specialists. There are some 4,000 Great Commission global networks. Millions of electronic messages and data files ostensibly related to the Great Commission flash across these networks around the globe everyday.'[1] Churches of all shapes and sizes, theologies and motivations have been mobilised for action. Spiritual 'Star Wars' is on. As the action gets heated, a phrase from the fable 'Snow White and the Seven Dwarfs' comes to mind. 'Mirror, mirror, on the wall, who is the fairest of us all?', says the wicked step-mother to her mirror. Jealousy, pride and seeking to be the fairest twists her with a hatred that plots murder—she poisons Snow White. A community of dwarfs with no mirror, but with compassionate hearts, bring life back to Snow White.

There is a real danger that history may be repeating itself as we move into this Decade of Evangelism. Inasmuch as superior armies and gun power enabled Christian expansionism in the fifteenth century, are the resources of modern communication creating a new cultural and religious dominance? Will the computer screens and laser printers only serve to isolate the Church even further from the world? Is our frantic mission emphasis enabling us to talk faster and more fluently past each other and the world? It is significant to recall that the message that was heard, received and acted upon in the fifteenth century did not automatically mean Christian growth. In fact in places like Sri Lanka, the opposite was true. Etched into the memory of this nation is the description of the Christian mission enterprise headed by the Portuguese. 'They came with the Bible in one hand and the sword in the other.' (Mahavamsa) The British enterprise in New Zealand in the 1860s receives a similar comment. 'When missionaries came first, they had two ploughs, one for heaven and one for earth. The one for heaven was kept going before our eyes, the other kept out of sight.' (Ngati Maniapoto, 1860.) The churches and denominations then as now were embroiled in the 'who is the fairest of us all' game. The mission, the Gospel, the evangel, had to struggle through this cacophony of self-indulgence and propagation to be heard.

One is reminded of the disciples and the argument that broke out on the road to Jerusalem as to which one of them was the greatest. Jesus' response is to place a child in their midst—'the one who is least among you all is the one who is great' (Luke 9.48). The eternal Word still walks the road to Jerusalem and the disciples do not seem to have grasped the central thrust of Christ's mission and what he came to communicate.

The opposite of communication is not silence, but alienation

Whatever sound we make or do not make, we communicate. John Bluck, one time communications director for the World Council of Churches, makes this point well when he says:

communication is as fundamental a human process as breathing. From our earliest years, we learn hundreds of subtle ways to recognise

161

when it's happening and when it's interrupted, distorted or forced. To be in communication with each other is to be in communion, not only with each other, but also with the way God intended us to be in the world. The opposite of communication is not silence, but alienation. We are made to be a communicating people, living in community.[2]

One of the central truths of the Bible is that God who is revealed and worshipped is a God who communicates. God's mission is to communicate. The stories of creation, the epic historic events of the Exodus, the tragedy of the exile, the birth, life, death and resurrection of Christ, the life of the early Church, all reflect the belief that God communicates not in a spiritual vacuum, but in the world—in the joys and sorrows of the community. The God who spans all time, the alpha and the omega, communicates in and through time. The mission of the Church through the ages is a story of the Holy Spirit acting in the life of the community enabling it to communicate. In times of persecution and trial through the courage of its martyrs, in times of distress and desolation through its acts of mercy and its word of hope, the mission of the Church has been communicated to the world. But this is not the full story. In its captivity to political power, through events like the Crusades, it proclaimed a gospel that replaced the Cross of Love with the sword of hate. In its greed for power, its fear and insecurity, it communicated a God who kept people in slavery, subduing the human mind and body to a life far removed from the 'abundant life' promised in the Gospel. The Truth of the Gospel has continued to be communicated in spite of the constant misrepresentation and false idols that have plagued the mission of the Church. Make no mistake—we may not have been consciously aware of it, but we have communicated.

The large church within the big city with its amplifiers, and highly motivated outreach programmes, communicates its understanding of mission, as does a small church in a depopulated rural community which is confused, anxious and uncertain of its future. Our very existence communicates to the world who we believe in, and how that belief impacts upon our lives.

162

As we have moved into the Decade of Evangelism, theologians have quite rightly pushed the Church to ask some prior questions. Why communicate? What is mission? What is it that motivates us to mission and communication?

Rediscovery of eschatology—the end things . . .

In a search for answers to these questions there has been a rediscovery of the place of eschatology. The truth regarding the end time. The doctrine of eschatology gives communication and mission its right focus. It puts God as the prime initiator and power behind all our activity. William J. Abraham, in his book *The Logic of Evangelism* states:

> whatever Evangelism may be, it is intimately related to eschatology. Eschatology is not just an esoteric theory about the last things. Within the Christian tradition, it is also an account of the pneumatic action of God in history in which God begins to realise those intentions that will be accomplished completely when he brings history to a close and establishes a new heaven and a new earth. Eschatology is a vision of the coming of the Kingdom of God that was initiated in Jesus of Nazareth, was experienced and cherished by the community that arose after his death and resurrection, and is now within the grasp of those who will repent and receive the gift of the Holy Spirit; yet it remains to come in all its glory and fullness. If this vision is correct, then there is good news for the world, there is indeed a Gospel worth sharing. Moreover, evangelism is an activity of the followers of Jesus that should be rooted and grounded in this dynamic, mysterious, numinous reality of the rule of God in history.[3]

Worship must be at the heart of mission and communication

One of the most significant consequences of rediscovering this truth and establishing its priority is that it gives worship the central place it deserves in the mission and life of the Church. It puts all our communication into perspective.

> One of the primary and irreplaceable ingredients in evangelism is the quality of worship in the Christian community. In this critical area,

163

the willingness to acknowledge and celebrate the inauguration of the rule of God is tested in a fundamental way. If God is not celebrated and adored as Lord in worship, it is highly unlikely that God's rule will be celebrated and welcomed anywhere else. Without a deep sense of the reality of God in the regular, liturgical life of the church, talk about initiating people in the rule of God will be vacuous and empty. Worship releases the Church to relax; it makes her aware that God is the primary agent in evangelism; it breaks the temptation to manipulate for worthy ends; and sets her free to mediate the presence of God and his rule.[4]

The disciple exiled on the isle of Patmos places this vision before us in poetic majesty as the angels and elders, heaven and earth are caught up in the worship of God. 'Holy, Holy, Holy, is the Lord God Almighty, who was and is and is to come' (Rev. 4.8). 'You are worthy, our Lord and our God, to receive glory and honour and power, for you created all things, and by your will they existed and were created' (Rev. 4.11).

'And I heard every creature in heaven and on earth and under the earth, and in the sea and all therein saying "To him who sits upon the throne and to the Lamb be blessing and honour and glory and might for ever and ever". And the four living creatures said "Amen" and the elders fell down and worshipped' (Rev. 5.13-14).

Worship enables us to focus on God's reign

This focus on worship moves us from a preoccupation with institutional growth that makes us look like some public relations company hired to do a professional job. It challenges us to be servants of God's kingdom. The world of the market place works on the basis of competing for the allegiance of women, men and children to the products it places before them. 'How many people can we hold by manipulative skills to hear our message and succumb to our power' is their prime motivation and objective. The Church through its worship is made to ask 'How many people has God called us to serve?'. Worship communicates to us that the mission is

God's, the Agenda is God's, and the Church's mission is possible only in partnership with God as we seek to invite people into accepting the reign of God. The vision of Isaiah the prophet, in Isaiah 6. 1-9, whose mission and call to communicate is totally immersed in the worship of God, must serve as a constant reminder to us of the centrality of worship in all we are called to be and do. This focus enables evangelism to be seen in its right perspective.

Evangelism cannot be the primary activity and preoccupation of the Church as if everything revolved around it like the earth revolves around the sun. This coveted position belongs to the kingdom of God. The kingdom of God must be the primary, unconditional priority of the Church, which exists in and for the coming of the rule of God in history. Only as she exists in and for that kingdom is she authentic and valid. Evangelism is important only because the kingdom is important; it is subordinate to the kingdom. Only because evangelism involves initiating people into the kingdom of God does it deserve our attention, our allegiance, and our very best endeavours. Only as we keep evangelism utterly subordinate to the dynamic rule of God are we liberated to participate in it with appropriate joy and confidence. To make evangelism the primary concern of the Church is to give it a misplaced and exaggerated position in our lives. The first task of the Church is to worship; to bow down before the Lord of glory, to celebrate God's love and majesty, and to invite God to rule over the length and breadth of all creation.[5]

The end times hijacked . . .

Unfortunately, eschatology has been hijacked by some Christians who see it as God's way of getting back at those who refuse to accept the invitation to acknowledge God's reign. Worse still it has fuelled a fear of the future. Armageddon, the catastrophe of a third world war, events in the Middle East, famines, earthquakes, seem to be pushed to fit perfectly into a belief in biblical prophesy. This concept of the end time only dilutes this prophetic tradition. A right understanding of the 'end things' will enable us to recognise that it is God who initiates, enables and will bring to completion the mission task. Making dates for the end of the world may be an exciting pastime, but it detracts from what we are called to be.

> The Church did not begin its evangelistic activity because it was terrified about the prospects that faced those who died without hearing about Christ. The Gospel spread and the Church grew because the sovereign hand of God was in the midst of the community that found itself surrounded by people who were puzzled and intrigued by what they saw happening. The overwhelming impression created by the traditions witnessing to the early evangelistic activity of the disciples is that the Holy Spirit was present in the community, bringing in the reign of God and inspiring the disciples to speak boldly of the mighty acts of salvation that God had wrought through the life, death, and resurrection of Jesus. The signs and wonders associated with the ministry of Jesus and to which Jesus introduced his disciples continued in the early community. The first converts gathered around the disciples and met together in the temple and in their homes for teaching, prayer, praise, fellowship, mutual care and the breaking of bread (Acts 2.42). They proclaimed the word about Jesus boldly, and when martyrdom and persecution drove them out of Jerusalem, they continued to wait upon the guidance of God and gossiped the good news of the kingdom to those who would listen. In other words, evangelism was rooted in a corporate experience of the rule of God that provided not only the psychological strength and support that was clearly needed in a hostile environment, but that also signified the active presence of God in their midst.[6]

In Christ all things cohere ...

The further importance of eschatology is that it holds together the personal and the corporate dimensions of faith in the mission of the Church. This enables us to communicate a faith that holds the story and its proclamation together with the invitation to worship and be nurtured in the community. It pushes us out to be servants of the Kingdom in acts of compassion and gives us the strength to walk into the hostile arena where the transformation of unjust structures becomes a consequence not of ideology, but of worship.

Whenever the Church communicates a fragmented and split gospel that focuses solely on individual piety (the private and confidential label worn by many Anglicans within the English speaking world) or on the civic Christian—duty to the neighbour is all that matters—or the political agitator who seeks the kingdom by eradicating the causes of injustice, it loses its vision of the 'end in God' and short-changes the Church and the world with a compartmentalised gospel that allows for consumer satisfaction, but diminishes the wholeness of Christ. 'Recovery and a firm grasp of a true doctrine of the last things, of eschatology' as Lesslie Newbigin suggests, is a firm essential in how we communicate the Gospel in this divided world.[7]

Mission must be grounded in the truth of the incarnation

Together with the rediscovery of eschatology, one of the necessary contributions that Anglicans can make is our emphasis on mission being grounded in the truth of the incarnation. The incarnation tells us of a God who communicates through the costly act of total identification with the human race. It portrays a respect and integrity for all who come in contact with the Divine Word. The local context and culture of the people are taken seriously and the Divine Word makes efforts to communicate in the language and symbol of the time. Writing to the Church in Colossae St Paul decribes the nature of the one who is incarnate.

> Christ is the image of the invisible God, the first-born of all creation; for in him all things were created, in heaven and on earth, visible and invisible, whether thrones or dominions or principalities or authorities—all things were created through him and for him. He is before all things, and in him all things hold together. He is the head of the

body, the Church; he is the beginning, the first-born from the dead, that in everything he might be pre-eminent. For in him all the fullness of God was pleased to dwell, and through him to reconcile to himself all things, whether on earth or in heaven, making peace by the blood of his cross. (Col. 1.15-20).

The extent of the involvement of the Christ in our world is summed up in one of the earliest hymns of the Church.

Have this mind among yourselves, which is yours in Christ Jesus, who, though he was in the form of God, did not count equality with God a thing to be grasped, but emptied himself, taking the form of a servant, being born in the likeness of men. And being found in human form he humbled himself and became obedient unto death, even death on a cross. Therefore God has highly exalted him and bestowed on him the name which is above every name, that at the name of Jesus every knee should bow, in heaven and on earth and under the earth, and every tongue confess that Jesus Christ is Lord, to the glory of God the Father (Phil. 2.5-11).

This act of self-giving—'kenosis'—is how God communicates. The incarnation portrays for us the way in which we must enact and embody the Great Commission to 'Go therefore and make disciples . . .' (Matt. 28.19). The incarnation tells us to respond to the need of the hearer rather than our own concerns. It reminds us of the sacredness of communication.

Communication is always a negotiation between sender and receiver, filtered through whatever channels are available, subject to hundreds of factors beyond our control or consciousness, shaped by context and culture, place, time and history. We long to jump free of all these constraints, to speak directly and make our true intentions clear, to see not darkly as through a glass, but face to face. Our reluctance to accept the slow and patient discipline that good communication demands suggests that secretly we think religious people deserve an easier, less mediated and more direct way to speak and be heard. Perhaps if we push the right button and choose the right pair, the Holy Spirit will do it for us. And that's a curious hope to foster in a people who believe God shows incarnation through a carpenter's son in a backwater town to show what life is all about.[8]

Incarnation allows for the working out of the fourfold nature of mission as described by the Anglican Consultative Council (ACC 6)—Proclamation, Nurture, Compassion, Transformation within the local context. Here the community of faith communicates by its 'being', by its interaction within itself and the community. Incarnation refuses to communicate in a dualism that creates a world out there to which we take God—God's reign has already begun. The incarnation makes God's presence visible in a language and form that enables us to say 'Yes'.

One of the consequences of our belief in the God who communicates through the incarnation process is the radical change that will be required in how we proclaim the message of the Gospel in word and symbol. If we imagine that the Decade of Evangelism will leave us as 'we were in the beginning, now and ever shall be, the same Church as forever' then we had better get off the communication wheel and build up our defences for the keeping of the old establishment. Change will come. Our understandings of the Church, the present models of ministry, the sacraments, the structures of our Synods and councils will be challenged. Mission based on the God of the incarnation will demand a participatory form of community life and a movement away from the hierarchical pattern of authority and decision making we have copied from the secular world. We will have to go through the difficult process of interpreting the timeless truths held in the thought patterns of another era into the framework of the twenty-first century. The sacrifice of Christ, the blood that saves, the body and the blood given for us, the wages of sin, law and grace, the word become flesh, to name but a few of our sacred truths will need to be reformulated to enable our generation to discover and respond to the truth of God in Christ. The experience of a Franciscan friar addressing a school assembly highlights the need for change. Speaking to the students about the various persecutions that Paul had undergone, he focused on 2 Corinthians 11.25 'Once I was stoned'. The whole assembly broke up into fits of laughter. Communication had happened, but it was not about rocks being thrown at Paul. The word 'stoned' to these young people meant only one thing and that was the experience that came from the use of certain drugs This simple illustration

169

indicates our need to find new ways of telling the old story. In many cultures, body and blood symbolises cannibalism. A god who demands a human sacrifice, however wonderful the saving consequences may be, does not meet with approval. This challenging art of reinterpreting the Gospel, to enable those who hear it to receive it in a way that they can respond, has been with the community of the scriptures from its very inception. The reflective process seen in the Gospel narratives displays subtle differences that enhance communication. In our own time and in our own generation, we will be required to be no less faithful if we are serious about our hearers and their response.

> The challenge for contemporary evangelists is to borrow and adapt secular images as boldly and imaginatively as earlier preachers and teachers that we have long since enshrined as thoroughly sacred. St Augustine for example introduced a whole new secular vocabulary to the Church of his time more earthy, vulgar, informal and entertaining than anything his contemporaries dared to employ. But it quickly became sanctified and for today's ears sounds holy and remote. Secular symbols, especially well televised ones that describe the natural world, or struggles for peace and justice that promote dignity and respect for women and men, black and white alike, portrayals of relationships that show love and consistency, celebrations of good humour and great beauty, all these secular statements and a thousand others can speak implicitly of God's mystery and love alive and incarnate in the world. In a society that has lost its fluency in the language of the sacred, such secular symbols, however indirect and understated they may be for evangelism, are certainly the first way and sometimes the only way left for talking about God.[9]

The Anglican Church in Canada has shown us an example of what is possible in the use of effective images that touch the point of concern and need of today's society. It portrays a Church that is contemporary with a story to tell and a faith to share. One of their newspaper advertisements is shown below.

Advertisement appearing in the *Anglican Journal*, Vol. 116, No. 9, November 1990

If it's not running right, speak with the original owner.

Now that you're recycling your paper, returning your containers, reusing your scrap and composting your waste, you might want to join others in praying for this green earth God gave us. If it's worth saving, isn't it worth praying for?

Show your spirit. Come back to church.

The Anglican Church

Media images were used to project the Church as a community not separate from the world, but one that lives alongside humanity, sharing their fears and hopes. People were invited to respond to the mystery of God through a creative use of the mass media.

The Bishop of Bathurst, Australia, the Rt Rev. Bruce Wilson, makes this plea for the Church.

> Whether it's toothpaste or McDonalds, or the Church, if it doesn't have a media image, it's not part of the 'perceived reality' that we all share, and it ceases to be an option. The media lets us comprehend who we are as a nation. On a parish level, too, we need to keep the rumour of God alive through our local newspapers and other media outlets. This task must be tackled at every level.[10]

We should not be captive to modernity, or its idols, but at the same time we must not be afraid to use the symbols and vehicles of communication that are common to the people of our time in order for the Gospel claims to be made through and by them.

Mission held in the womb of expectancy and waiting

The truth of the incarnation also holds mission and communication in the womb of expectancy and waiting. It takes us away from the desire that we must be hyperactive. Cracking the whip will never get people into the kingdom. One of the real problems in modern communication is the desire to sensationalise every little facet of information. It prods and pushes and keeps the information flowing at a pace that makes it difficult both to receive and to respond in a meaningful way. It makes us feel helpless and hopeless. The so-called compassion fatigue that has entered into the minds and hearts of several TV viewers is a direct consequence of the overload of information on matters surrounding critical areas of human need. Modern technological communication lives on the 'move on to the next business' principle, some other sensational story, newsbreak or issue that is perceived by the media to be important rolls up to grab our attention before the picture of the last scene has faded. How then does one seek to keep the truth of the incarnation in a world that trivialises the important? Raymond Fung of the Council for World Mission and Evangelism, whose writings on mission, evangelism and communication are perceptive and inspiring, has some helpful pointers in this regard. He says:

> No evangelism can be authentic without mystical communion with God on the part of the evangelist in a posture of expectancy and

awaiting. Mystical theology, by whatever different names it is known, is present in all Christian traditions. It affirms contemplation, prayer and waiting, as ways of knowing God and of drawing people to Christ. I think we need to grasp at the outset that waiting is an attitude, an inclination to act. As we wait, we communicate that life is not all that it should be. We wait because there is something there which is worth having. Also, we wait because the resources we need to survive and to grow have not been given to our keeping. We wait because we have hope. The theological mandate for evangelistic waiting is not hard to discern. Christians need to wait because God waits. In waiting, we partake in God's nature. And, how God waits informs our own waiting. Jesus waits for Peter to weep and return. For Thomas to join the disciples and set aside his doubt. Jesus waits for the two travellers to recognise him on the Emmaus Road. We need to wait for the human heart to catch up with Jesus. Furthermore, Christians are asked to pray for Jesus' return, for the kingdom to come in all of its abundance. The Christian life must therefore be a life lived in the posture of waiting, of expectancy that God will do wonders, maybe through us, perhaps through others.[11]

Fung suggests that in the secular community that we are living in, there is a growing inclination for people to inch their way back to the Christian faith. In this process they are whispering some of the deepest questions to us. 'Do you know God?'

If they sense that we do not, because of our busyness or because we haven't really listened to their question, then they will go away again, perhaps this time more sadly than cynically. And if they sense that we do, it will not be because we say we do. It will because they see it in the way we live, in the manner of our speaking, and in our willingness to listen and to search. They will see it in the freedom this knowledge provides and in what this knowledge commits us to.

The second reason Fung suggests

in the dynamic waiting for evangelistic thinking and action is the tremendous prospect for the intellectual re-orientation of theology, for the spiritual renewal of the churches and for a vigorous missionary thrust among the oppressed and the suffering people of the earth. The key lies in a simple observation. Waiting is part of the culture of the poor. We all know that poor people wait. Wealthy and powerful people do not wait. This is true anywhere. Waiting tells the degrees of power and wealth. In fact, the rat race for wealth and power, on a personal or national level, can be fairly satisfactorily explained by this one desire—the desire to not wait, and to have others wait for us and on us. So, if evangelism requires waiting and the poor have a lot of experience with that, then common sense requires that the whole church turn its eyes, tune its ears, gear its attention to the poor and start from there.[12]

The Cross judges our mission efforts . . .

Mission and communication in this Decade of Evangelism will be tempted by the dazzling lights of technological advancement in the area of mass communication. There are segments of this vast resource that we should be able to use wisely and well for the proclamation of the Gospel. To believe, however, that the wonder of scientific achievement and our use of it will initiate people into the kingdom of God is to reject the doctrine of eschatology and incarnation which need to be at the centre of both our mission and our desire to communicate.

Towering over the wrecks of our weak attempts to communicate the Gospel—living through the ravages of time is a symbol which brings out the heart of our mission—the Cross—a horrible yet glorious paradox. This paradox must inspire and judge our every effort, our words and actions. It has often been misused but it continues to confront us. It beckons us never to trivialise our mission. Let one of the communicators of the first century speak.

For we do not proclaim ourselves; we proclaim Jesus Christ as Lord and ourselves as your slaves for Jesus' sake. (2 Cor. 4.5).

We have this treasure in clay jars, so that it may be made clear that this extraordinary power belongs to God and does not come from us. (2 Cor. 4.7).

We proclaim Christ crucified a stumbling block to the Jews and foolishness to the Gentiles . . . Yet God's foolishness is stronger than human wisdom and God's weakness is stronger than human strength (1 Cor 1.22-25).

May I never boast of anything except the Cross of our Lord Jesus

Christ by which the world has been crucified to me and I to the world (Gal 6.14).

Roger and Out...

When the story of this Decade of Evangelism is told by those who have been at the receiving end of our communications, what would their 'Roger and out' mean? Message received, understood, acted upon. Will it tell of a mission and communication that is true to the Gospel of the self-giving, eternally patient, compassionate God who in Christ is available to all, or will it reflect an institutional battle for survival or expansion that is perceived by those who receive it as a continuing exploitation, degrading and destruction of the powerful over the powerless, a betrayal of all that is precious in the Gospel of the wounded and risen Christ?

The Gospel is God's most precious gift freely given to us. The Cross proclaims God's love for the world. Our mission and communication must be fired by God's love and must ever stand under the mercy and judgement of the Cross. We travel this journey into this Decade aware that God in Christ walks before us and with us, that God's spirit will change and tranform us, so that God may be glorified.

Notes

1. *International Bulletin*, p.20, David P. Barrett, 1989 Statistical Table.
2. *Speak or Squeak*, John Bluck, p. 6.
3. *The Logic of Evangelism*, William J. Abraham, Eerdmans, p. 38.
4. Ibid., p. 168.
5. Ibid., p. 182.
6. Ibid., p. 38.
7. *Foolishness to the Greeks*, Lesslie Newbigin, WCC Mission Series, p. 133.
8. *Speak or Squeak*, John Bluck, p. 7.
9. Ibid., pp. 14,15.
10. *Anglican News* Vol. 8 No. 3., p. 3.
11. 'Thinking Mission—Waiting—the Strategic Art of Evangelism', Raymond Fung, *Network*, USPG, Oct. 1990, Issue 4.
12. Ibid., Fung.

EPILOGUE:
A STORY TO TELL

Gideon Olajide

I will begin this section with the words of the opening verse of Edward J. Burn's hymn 'Good News'. The opening verse reads:

> We have a gospel to proclaim,
> good news for all throughout the earth:
> the gospel of a Saviour's name:
> we sing his glory, tell his worth.

The focus of this book has been to highlight:

   (i) the components of holistic mission and their relationship to evangelism
  (ii) mission in context
 (iii) the necessary shift of the posture of the church from maintenance to mission

I will now corroborate what these writers have stated theologically with real life stories which are the outcome of grass roots evangelism and the outpouring of the Holy Spirit as God's people bear faithful witness in context. My experience is that God's people know God's blessing when they are obedient to the Holy Spirit.

Case Studies

a. Directly after our Ibadan Diocese synod meeting in mid-May 1991, a group of young evangelists in one of our inner city churches responded to the urge of the Holy Spirit in response to the call to put the vision of the Decade of Evangelism into immediate action. They were moving into a rural area where there are still pockets of unreached groups or at best nominal Christians. With the economic situation in the country as it is, their immediate problem was transportation. They could not

177

afford to buy a bus. In the face of apparent odds they embarked on the move prayerfully trusting their needs to the Lord. To their joy and surprise while they were praying, an anonymous donor delivered to them a new bus given specifically for evangelism in the remote rural areas of the dioceses. They received this gift from the Lord while they were yet praying and hoping for some cash gift to help their transport fare. Our God answers prayer and *surprises* his people with miracles.

b. In response to the proclamation of the gospel, people accept Jesus as Lord and Saviour and show this in their Christian living and witness. Three such people saw themselves drawn to one another because of the new life they had found in Jesus. They began a group for Bible study and prayer in a room at the government administrative headquarters. By their second meeting, nine people were in attendance. By their third meeting they were twenty-seven. Today they are over *700* and have grown into a fellowship working to own a worship centre, a cafeteria, a baby-minding centre and nursery school. They reach out to hospitals and prisons and village churches around them. They share their faith with courage and a few of them are persecuted because they dare to be the salt of the earth in an environment full of corrupt practices.

c. Miracles of healing occur as a consequence of obedience to the Great Commission. Last year four members of a youth forum were moved during an evangelistic meeting to leave the place of prayer in church and go out to pray for a crippled boy not far away from the church gate. They obeyed and were surprised because the Lord gave respect to their prayer and courageous obedience by lifting up the cripple. He is a member of the church today. The boys were no experts in faith healing nor has that sort of thing happened to them again since last year, but the event brought renewal to the worship life and the personal commitment of members of the church.

d. Each of the older churches in the city of Lagos sponsored the founding of a missionary diocese in the northern part of Nigeria in 1990, thus enabling the Archbishop to establish ten missionary dioceses in one year. They continue to nurture these dioceses.

e. I have had the joy of fellowship with either individuals or groups of Christians who have passed through the harrowing experience of the burning of churches and killing or maiming of people and destruction of properties in some parts of my country. They have come out of it as better Christians and more determined and effective evangelists, having been purified by the fire of affliction and persecution. Unlike many of us who are, as it were, at 'ease in Zion', they have known in unmistakable experience the truth of the verse of the hymn, 'Jesus, I my cross have taken, all to leave and follow thee'. They know that when all ambition, all they have sought, all they have hoped, all they have known has perished, they can still say:

> yet how rich is my condition
> God and heaven are still my own.
> Men may trouble and distress me
> 'Twill but drive me to your breast,
> life with trials hard may press me,
> Heaven will bring me sweeter rest.
> Oh, 'tis not in grief to harm me
> while thy love is left to me.
> Oh 'twere not in joy to charm me
> were that joy unmixed with thee.

Non-Christians have become Christians through the witness of these living martyrs, as they were led to ask what power sustained them that *they did not retaliate* when they were physically assaulted and tortured. They had to let the enquirers know that it was the power that Jesus supplied and which they too could have if they submitted their lives to Jesus as their Lord and Saviour.

f. To further the process of evangelism, the Lambeth Conference calls for the overhaul of structures. When we yield in total obedience to the leading of the Holy Spirit, we will become in his hands 'those that have turned the world upside down' for good (Acts 17:6). As one reads the news of the goings on in South Africa today one rejoices at how the Lord has prospered the labours of those who in obedience were the agents and instruments of the change.

An incident happened at Amsterdam at the International Congress of Itinerant Evangelists in 1986. For lack of accommodation at that congress, I had to share a bed with a white South African overnight. He dodged going to sleep for a long time and when he did finally, he must have slept for only an hour or two. He woke me up to share with me the dealings of the Lord with him. Expositions of the scriptures at the congress had brought renewal to his life and transformed him. He said that in the light of the teaching of Matt. 5.23-26, white South African Christians are the ones to take the initiative to dismantle apartheid. He was going home to lead the crusade for this as he has been given this new insight. Before dawn he had packed his baggage; he could not wait for breakfast; he found the first available plane back home. We are today reaping the fruit of the labours of many like him who were not disobedient to the heavenly vision given to them.

I have chosen these rather unrelated events to encourage those who still nurse genuine misgivings about the Decade of Evangelism, that such misgivings may be misplaced as they may be reactions to only one aspect or methodology of evangelism. We must be careful not just to talk it to death and then become like those who say 'Lord, Lord', but fail to do the will of our heavenly Father.

The call for a Decade of Evangelism from different Churches and denominations and para-church organisations at this period in history is God's visitation in redemption to his Church and world. As at the first Pentecost, dreams and visions which God gave to individuals and groups, he now lavishes on 'all flesh' internationally, and inter-denominationally (Joel 2.28ff; Acts 2.17ff).

Individualism in evangelism is giving way to sharing of ministries within the Communion and ecumenically, and the specialist approach is being overtaken by collective witness of which every church member feels a part. Love, humility and reliance on the Holy Spirit are overcoming intolerance and arrogance. Our God is on the move through his Church and will fulfil his purposes.

One of the purposes is that the Church shift from maintenance to mission. This will no doubt affect the administrative structures among other things.

This may mean more empowerment of the laity for fuller and freer participation in evangelism and other aspects of the ministry of the Church and, certainly, greater emphasis on discipleship and consistent Christian living so as to match numerical growth with spiritual maturity and depth of knowledge.

(a) The Laity

Hitherto, because of our inheritance of a clergy-centred Church, the laity have played second fiddle in the area of evangelism. Yet the contact of the clergy with the masses is minimal. The laity are the ones who live on the frontier, who mix most easily with non-Christian workmates, neighbours and friends. They are the ones who are able to extend the frontiers of the Church. The future of the Church and her evangelistic work therefore lies with the laity. Seen in this way, the bishop's role becomes that of focal point for unity and the source of inspiration in evangelism and pastoral care for the whole community of the people of God acting in concert.

(b) Voluntary Agencies

Credit will always be given to voluntary societies and agencies who have been the handmaid of the Church in fulfilling the Great Commission over the centuries. They themselves have felt the need for partnership with one another. They have been like David's men of war, mighty, able giants as individuals. The greatest qualification of David's men was not what they were as individuals but *what they were together*. They were 'men of war who can keep rank' (1 Chron. 12.38). My point here, therefore, is that missionary societies of the Communion should work in closer co-operation with one another and look forward to a merger into a 'federation' for more effective and unduplicated ministry. This will not only save money and resources, it will itself become an evangelistic message, for our unity is at once our source of strength and a means of conversion for the watching world.

(c) Sharing of Ministries

Our theology of giving should be in the light of Matt 5.43-48 and 1 John 3.16ff. We have a lot to learn from Islam, which manifests a more Christian theology of giving than we. In the sharing of

God's wealth, the Muslims behave more like the Church in Antioch in relation to the Church in Jerusalem or like the Church in Macedonia also sharing with the Church in need. Part of the mission of the Church in a selfish world is to lead the way in selfless sharing and equitable redistribution of God-given wealth so that among us there is no-one lacking in whatever is needed to make life viable (Acts 4.34-35).

As this millennium draws to its end, the Lord has led the Church into accepting the challenge to make its closing years a Decade of Evangelism. This gives every member of the Church the opportunity *by word and deed* (including if necessary by what each suffers) to communicate the gospel of Christ. Thus we have a story to tell as we:

> Tell the praise of him who called us
> Out of darkness into light,
> Broke the fetters that enthralled us,
> Gave us freedom, peace and sight:
> Tell the tale of sins forgiven,
> Strength renewed and hope restored,
> Till the earth, in tune with heaven,
> Praise and magnify the Lord.
>
> (*C. A. Alington*)

Amen. Maranatha.